The Epistles to the Philippians, Colossians, and Philemon

The Epistles to the Philippians, Colossians, and Philemon

by
Paul S. Rees

BAKER BOOK HOUSE
Grand Rapids, Michigan
1964

Library of Congress Catalog Card Number: 64-14823

PHOTOLITHOPRINTED BY CUSHING - MALLOY, INC.
ANN ARBOR, MICHIGAN, UNITED STATES OF AMERICA
1 9 6 4

Editor's Foreword

In the series, Proclaiming the New Testament, an attempt is made to provide homiletical comments and ideas. The busy pastor needs to spend time in meditation if he is to offer the bread of life to his people. One of the best known methods of Bible study is to work through one book of the Bible at a time. This gives depth as well as breadth. It provides for the preaching of the whole counsel of God and not just a part of that revelation. As truth must reach people in various stages of growth and at different levels of reception, so there must be variety of communication.

The intention of this series is to stimulate men in the ministry to more definite study. Believing that the first rule of homiletics is to read and study the actual text of Scripture, this method brings ideas and suggestion. Here illustrations are limited as the individual should find his own as he reads or mingles with people, and as he is open to all the winds of God. No pastor can lead his people to a level of thought and spiritual experience higher than the one he occupies. God will not honor lazy men or men who imagine the Holy Spirit should prompt alone. God has given us a mind to use, a heart to love, a spirit to pray, and a will to study.

These results are possible from this approach. *One,* the pastor and student will find suggestive ideas. As Charles H. Spurgeon said of William Gurnall (1616-79), a Puritan, "I have found his work the best thought-breeder in all our library. I should think more discourses have been suggested by it than by any other. I have often resorted to it when my own fire has been burning low. . . ." *Two,* the user will see how to study an entire book of the Bible for preaching values. *Three,* the man of God will be encouraged to begin the study of the Bible book for himself and find by this method other treasures of homiletical insight.

While using the King James or Authorized Version, the student should compare with all other versions and translations as well as the original text when available.

Many and varied are the commentaries available for the profit of the preacher. These include the following:

I. *Critical.* This deals with the text in the light of biblical criticism, seeking to apply historical principles and a rational approach to the text, e.g., *The International Critical Commentary, the Moffatt New Testament Commentary, The Expositor's Greek Testament,* and the commentaries of H. A. W. Meyer, and Keil and Delitsch.

II. *Exegetical.* This seeks to lead out the exact meaning of the text in terms of the words and idioms in the light of their background and use originally, e.g., *The Westminster Commentaries, the New International Commentary on the New Testament, The Evangelical Commentary on the New Testament,* and the commentaries of R. C. H. Lenski, J. P. Lange, and W. Hendriksen.

III. *Expository.* This expounds and applies the dominant theme of each section or unit in the light of history and with relevance to the present, e.g., *The Expositor's Bible, The Interpreter's Bible, Calvin's Commentaries, The Pulpit Commentary,* and *An American Commentary on the New Testament.*

IV. *Devotional.* This brings out the inner sense or the spiritual essence as applied to the soul in meditation. Here is the stimulus to the spiritual life of the believer, e.g., *A Devotional Commentary,* and Matthew Henry's *Commentary on the Whole Bible.*

The present type of book is neither a Bible study book nor a book of outlines. It is not a commentary as the above. We seek to encourage the preacher to engage in the reading and studying of the book to find the homiletical units. As "the servant of the Word" let him work toward this ideal:

the Historical setting,
the Expository meaning,
the Doctrinal value,
the Practical aim,
the Homiletical form

The First Presbyterian Church
of Seattle, Washington

Ralph G. Turnbull
General Editor

• • • • • • • • • • • • , • • • •

Introduction

Three matters are on my mind:

1. *The significance of the word "proclaiming in the general title of this series.* The gospel is news. It is eminently *publishable.* If in our treatment of it it loses this character, the fault is ours, not the gospel's. Never far from my mind, therefore, has been the remembrance that what is being written is designed to be a spur and an aid to those whose fortunate task it is to stand before congregation, or Sunday School class, or study group, and *proclaim* the manifold riches of the Christian message. John Wycliffe, in acceptable fourteenth century English usage, said that he wanted to translate the Bible in a "language understanded of the people." This indeed is how you and I are to *preach* and *teach the* Bible's grand message.

2. *The immeasurable value to preachers and teachers of having minds that are saturated with Holy Scripture.* I know that familiarity with rules of interpretation is important. I do not forget that a grasp of the Bible's structural ideas and their unfolding, its key events and their significance, is urgently necessary. But I know also that too frequently the responsibility for Biblical proclamation and instruction is in the hands of those whose minds are not immersed in Scripture. The claim has been made — let no one suppose that I have personally verified it — that in the volumes of sermons left to posterity by St. John Chrysostom there are seven thousand quotations from the Old Testament and eleven thousand from the New. It is hoped that, among other desirable ends, this examination of three Pauline epistles will serve to stimulate an insatiable hunger to know the Bible — a very different thing, it should be added, from knowing *about* the Bible.

3. *The magnificent variety and balance, both of truth and*

9

treatment, to be found in the writing of Paul, to which fact Philippians, Colossians, and Philemon bear excellent witness. In Philippians the relaxed mind of a grateful friend employing every shade and nuance of courtesy to do justice to his delicate feelings! In Colossians the intense stretch-out of a phenomenal theological intelligence, soaring to the heights, plumbing the depths, of sublime Christology! In slender Philemon the incredibly skillful handling of a private affair between a master and his run-away slave! And all of it so informed by the authority of the Holy Spirit of God, and so relevant to a thousand human situations, that the Church Universal has cherished it as irreplaceable!

Bishop Westcott said of Origen that he seemed to hold the whole of Scripture in solution in his mind. If this volume makes even a small contribution to an achievement so worthy, I shall regard as abundantly worthwhile the work that has gone into its preparation.

Finally, I deem it fitting to offer my very warm thanks to two Christian groups with which I have close and meaningful relationship and on whose fraternal bounty I trustingly lean:

1. To the Evangelical Covenant Church of America, custodian under God of my ordination vows, for giving me its blessing in the wide-ranging inter-church ministry in which it is currently mine to engage, and

2. To World Vision, Inc., which, through its distinguished president, Dr. Bob Pierce, gives its encouragement to my *written,* no less than my *spoken,* ministry.

I wish to acknowledge my indebtedness to Harper and Row, Publishers, Incorporated, for permission to quote from Charles Clayton Morrison's book, *Can Protestantism Win America?* (1948).

In this seventh decade of my life I find that, resting more heavily upon me than ever, is the sheer weight of indebtedness for favors undeserved.

Paul S. Rees

World Vision, Inc.
International Headquarters
Pasadena, California

Contents

The Epistle to the Philippians

Philippians 1
PRAYER FOR PROGRESS

1:9. "And this I pray, that your love may abound yet more and more."

I. HISTORICAL SETTING. Paul, while in prison (probably in Rome, possibly at Ephesus, improbably at Caesarea) writes a letter of thanks, love, and solicitude to the Christians in Philippi. They have sent him a gift by Epaphroditus their messenger; and they will soon receive, at Epaphroditus' hand, this Epistle of cheerful, almost blitheful, gratitude. The Philippians were, in a bit of phrasing that comes back to me from a sermon heard years ago, "Paul's sweetheart church." If this sounds too saccharine, it nevertheless makes sense. These believers were the first fruits of the apostle in Europe. Bringing the gospel to them had been a costly venture. Acts 16:12-40 tells the story. It was at Philippi, which proudly flew the flag of a Roman free city, that Paul and Silas had been flogged half to death. It was here that they had been brutally jailed. From these birthpangs issued a precious child: "all the saints which are in Christ Jesus at Philippi, with the bishops and deacons" (1:1).

II. EXPOSITORY MEANING. 1:1. "Servants," from the Greek *douloi,* suggests submission without servility: the slavery is that of love, the service that of a willing spirit.

"Saints" in Paul's vocabulary are all those who, by faith, are "in Christ." These are the people of God under the New Covenant. They are "holy ones" in virtue of their relationship to Christ. Here the stress falls on *life* in Christ rather than *likeness* to Christ. The converse of this, in Pauline terminology, is "Christ in you," where the emphasis does indeed fall on our being fashioned into His likeness.

1:2. "Grace" and "peace." The one from the Greek world, the other from the Hebrew; the one speaking of *gift* and *good-will,* the other of *health* and *well-being;* and both linked with what God has done in Jesus Christ to show forth his lovingkindness and bestow His reconciling, health-giving mercy.

1:5. "Fellowship in the gospel" has its antecedent in the thanksgiving of verse 3. *Koinonia,* the word for fellowship, has become in our day almost as familiar as *agape.* The meaning is that of common interest and mutual participation. Context indicates that "in the gospel" may be taken to mean *in the furtherance of the gospel.*

1:6. "Begun" and "will perform" are from Greek words that, according to Lightfoot, have sacramental overtones. The image suggested is that of a sacrificial ritual initiated and completed. Accordingly, the "good work" would be, in Paul's mind, the Philippians' "co-operation with and affection for the Apostle." This is Lightfoot's view and these are his words. Matthew Henry sees here a reference to the planting of the church in Philippi, which was God's doing, and which He will "see through" to the consummation of Christ's return. Others speak of the "good work" as "growth in grace." Still others interpret it to mean the Christian life regarded as a whole.

1:8. "The bowels of Jesus Christ" is equivalent to *the heart of Jesus Christ.* The Greek *splagchna* means the upper intestines: heart, liver, lungs. Here, to the ancients, was the seat of the emotions.

1:9. The Greek word for love, *agape,* has become so familiar that it is all but "Anglicized." It is to be distinguished from the *erotic,* the *filial,* and the broadly *affectional* (e.g., "I *like* him"). Its Biblical meaning is much more closely linked with the *will* than with the *emotions.* It is good-will acting from motives which are supplied by itself and not found in the object toward which it is directed. Hence the close tie between "love" and "grace." *Agape* is good-will in self-surrender and self-sacrifice. If, as is often said, self-preservation is the first law of the natural order, self-giving is the first law of the supernatural order. For "love is of God" (I John 4:7) and "God is love" (I John 4:8).

"Your love." God's love for you, which you have embraced; your love for God, evoked by His for you; your love for me and for one another. It is all there. Highly refined distinctions which rule out one shade of meaning in favor of another should be avoided.

"Abound." *May continue to abound* is the force of the present progressive tense.

"Knowledge," the Greek *epignosis,* taken in context, speaks of advanced knowledge, with accent on the experimental rather than the academic, the practical rather than the theoretical.

"Judgment." Extraordinary sensitiveness and discernment in those areas of living where "knowledge" must be applied.

1:10. "That ye may approve things that are excellent" is one of two possible renderings of the Greek, the other being: "that ye may put to the proof the things that differ." "The discrimination of love applies tests and makes distinctions impossible to the untrained moral sense" (Vincent).

"Sincere," the Greek *eilikrines,* is uncertain as to derivation. It may mean *tested by the sunlight* or *sifted by revolution.* The "revolution" would be that of whirling as in a sifter. Moffatt, for example, using "transparent," leans to the first; the Revised Standard Version, using "pure," leans to the second. The New English Bible renders it "flawless," thus giving little clue as to whether one derivation or the other made any difference to the translators.

"Without offense," *aproskopoi,* may be rendered *not causing others to stumble* or *not stumbling.* "Blameless" is the word favored by most translators.

1:11. "The fruits of righteousness." The best manuscript authority favors the singular "fruit," well rendered by Moffatt and the New English Bible as "harvest." Thus it is best to think of Paul as meaning not a harvest which consists of righteousness but a harvest such as righteousness produces. Here is the practical output of that faith-righteousness of which the apostle will speak in 3:9. Faith alone saves us, but the faith that saves never remains alone: it works.

III. DOCTRINAL VALUE. Out of Paul's intercessory concerns for the Philippian church three doctrines emerge, at least in germ: (1) the doctrine of prayer, (2) the doctrine of love, and (3) the doctrine of growth. The New Testament offers a wealth of material with respect to each of them.

IV. PRACTICAL AIM. In an over-simplified manner of speaking, this epistle is simply a "thank you" from one Christian to a group of Christians. Paul is in prison. They have sent him a gift borne affectionately by one of their number. And now the recipient of the gift, always a thankful soul and a master of the art of courtesy, would say to them, "I am amply supplied by what you have sent by Epaphroditus, a fragrant perfume, the sort of sacrifice that God approves and welcomes" (4:18, Moffatt).

Linked with gratitude is concern. This concern takes the shape of prayer. Prayer is pious, we admit. Do we as readily admit that prayer is practical? True, it spoils prayer if we induce it or exercise it just for the "results" we can garner from it. Yet, given the living God and living men who long to have His will done, prayer becomes practically resultful in ways both assuring and astounding. Nor is this ever more dynamically true than when, as in Paul's case here, the prayer is a selfless, loving intercession for others. Prayer was annihilating space long before telephones and radio got around to it. As John Magee says, "To pray for a friend on another continent is as fruitful as to pray for a person in the next room. All of us have a kind of co-presence in God. In His Being we are intimately connected and have our true relationship with one another."[1] Prayer such as this is neither futile nor fatuous. It is efficiency of the highest order.

V. HOMILETICAL FORM

Theme: "Prayer for Progress."

---

[1] *Prayer and Reality* (New York: Harper and Brothers), p. 146.

Introduction: A. J. Gossip, of late Scottish preaching fame, tells of a day when he asked a devout and discerning layman what part of the worship service he found most helpful. The man's answer left no doubt that for him (and he knew it, Gossip said, to be true of many others) the supreme moment of the service was the Intercessory Prayer.

To such a moment and such a mood we are brought as this man Paul prays for the Christians in Philippi.

The burden of his prayer? Their development and enrichment in the life of Christian love. Here indeed is the pith and marrow of all Christian growth: "that your love may abound yet more and more."

Examine now the concerns that speak out in this prayer.

A. Here, obviously, is prayer that concerns itself with the *possession* of love.

It is "your love," but only by derivation. Actually, it is God's love *given* to you.

The gift was Christ — not a package but a Person! Receiving Him, you have received love. Paul and John agree: "Herein is love, not that we loved God, but that he loved us, and sent his Son to be the propitiation [or "atoning sacrifice," as the Berkeley Version has it] for our sins" (I John 4:10).

On any Christian scheme of interpretation, the love of which Paul speaks is no native product of the poisoned soil of man's nature. It is an exotic. It must be transplanted from God's heart to ours.

And this is what the gospel is all about: God is giver; man is receiver. That makes it *grace*. The very love with which we relate ourselves to Him in obedience and service has been evoked by His so-great-love for us. The barrier or alienation between us and Him has been removed by that act of reconciliation which He in love undertook in the death of Christ. The new equipment of motivation — something to live *for* beyond ourselves and beyond our means — He in love has provided.

All of this, in its revolutionary beginnings, had come home

to the hearts of these Philippian Christians before Paul ever wrote them a line. He knows it. They know it.

God's love in Christ has got hold of them. They are in possession of it.

But where to go from there — this is the apostle's pastoral concern!

B. Thus we come to the realization that here is prayer which concerns itself with the *progress* of love.

To have God's love *abiding* in us is much. To have it *abounding* in us is more. All the dynamic development of Paul's "more and more" comes into view here.

Love's growth is inseparable from what we *know*. Our love is to abound "in knowledge and in all judgment," or, as the New English Bible has it, it is to "grow ever richer in knowledge and insight of every kind."

"Love is blind," we say. As applied to our sentimental and sensual infatuations, yes; as applied to the self-giving goodwill we gain from Christ, no. Christ's *agape* working in us is neither an unregulated emotion nor an unenlightened mysticism. It is a particular craving for truth in which Christ is both our hunger and our bread, both the stimulator and the satisfier of our need.

Love's progress, moreover, is inseparable from what we *value*. Why should love move steadily toward increasing knowledge and sharper insight? Paul's answer: "So that you may approve what is excellent." Some translators prefer to render the Greek: "So that you may test the things that differ." On either rendering we come out at the same place: capacity for evaluation, ability to assess priorities, knowledgeable insistence that first things must come first. The preacher needs this, else he will put ecclesiastical niceties and promotional gimmicks ahead of solid prayer and the discipline of strong and relevant expository preaching. The layman needs this, else he will confuse committee work with devotedness to Christ and let himself "off the hook" by giving the church his money instead of giving God his heart.

Furthermore, love's growth is inseparable from what we *do*.

We are to be "filled with the fruits of righteousness which come through Jesus Christ to the glory and praise of God" (v. 11). If love cannot be scientifically proved (you cannot "capture" it in a test tube or "fix" it under a microscope), it can be practically demonstrated. Think how often in the New Testament this point is driven home:

"If ye know these things, happy are ye if ye do them."

"Herein is my Father glorified that ye bear much fruit."

"The fruit of the light is found in all that is good and true and right."

"If ye love me, ye will keep my commandments."

Wherever you turn on the shining pages of God's Book there is this insistence on the linking up of affection and action, faith and fruit, being and doing, doctrine and demonstration.

In Paul's writings Christians are not *idealized* (that is, portrayed as though they were without defect or deficiency), but, on the other hand they are *normalized* (that is, they are portrayed again and again as God intends them to be, and as indeed they can be, in virtue of their union with Jesus Christ by faith).

In such a portrayal it is notable that what Christians *are* and what they *do* have an intimacy of connection too often overlooked in today's church life. What is the norm here, according to Paul? It is redeemed humanity under the rule of Christ's love, open to all the insights and values which love growingly brings with it, and thus giving to the possessors of this love a quality that God calls "pure and blameless." Yet it must be quickly added that this purity, or singlemindedness, of love, far from being a "fugitive and cloistered virtue," is "filled with the fruits of righteousness."

A missionary in India needed physical assistance to get a critically sick man from his house to the hospital. She requested help from two "holy men" who were sitting not far away, intoning their devotions. She said she would never forget the fire of resentment that blazed up in the eyes of one of them, as he replied: "We? We are holy men. We never do anything for anybody."

Strangely twisted and dangerously false is any such concept of "holiness." Yet it would be adding complacency to complacency if we were to dismiss this incident as a sad example of heathen perversion. The ingrown, self-occupied triviality of much that passes for piety today needs blasting from our own slothful hearts.

"The fruits of righteousness!"

Dear God, fill us with them!

C. Here, finally, is prayer that concerns itself with the *prospect* of love.

Two phrases must have our attention: "the day of Christ" (v. 10) and "the glory and praise of God" (v. 11).

Consider the first. We are to go on approving "what is excellent" and being "pure and blameless," not simply "till," as the King James has it, but "for," as the Revised Standard has it, "the day of Christ." The Greek may be rendered *against,* or *with a view to.*

"The day of Christ" (twice used by the apostle in the first ten verses of the chapter) is specifically prophetic. It speaks of the return of Christ, with all the unveiling of triumph and lordship that will attend it. Listen to Robert Johnstone, distinguished Scottish expositor of the last century, in comment on this verse and phrase: "The coming of the Lord was to Paul no mere article of an orthodox creed, no mere necessary constituent of a complete confession of faith. It stood out before him as intensely real. The thought of it colored his whole being. Glowing love to Him who, in His first coming, had suffered and died . . . ; and a vivid realizing faith in His second coming, His glorious appearing to raise the dead, to judge the world, and introduce His people into the full blessedness and glory of salvation — these were plainly the moving springs of this great Christian's life."

They were indeed!

Now take the second phrase: "to the glory and praise of God." It is to this, as end and aim, that "the fruits of righteousness" in the life of growing love are always pointing.

How do the two prospects compare with each other? Let

us put it this way: for *inspiration,* love looks *ahead* to "the day of Christ." Meanwhile, for *incentive,* it looks *up* to "the glory and praise of God."

Let us be put on notice that righteousness divorced from love appears in many a guise. Look at the Pharisee in our Lord's story: making a parade of his virtue and looking down contemptuously upon the vile publican at his side. Here is righteousness which is to the glory and praise of its deceived professor. His righteousness, such as it is, is his own doing. Paradoxically, it becomes his own damnation. Not he, whose pride kept him in tragic alienation from God, but the man whom he despised, "went down to his house justified."

Then

> "Jesus, confirm my heart's desire
> To work, and speak, and think for Thee;
> Still let me guard the holy fire,
> And still stir up Thy gift in me.

> "Ready for all Thy perfect will,
> My acts of faith and love repeat,
> Till death Thy endless mercies seal,
> And make the sacrifice complete."

Philippians 1

WHEN DIFFICULTIES BECOME DOORS

1:12. "I would ye should understand, brethren, that the things which happened to me have fallen out rather unto the furtherance of the gospel."

I. HISTORICAL SETTING. If it cannot be proven beyond doubt, it can be reasonably presumed that the "bonds" to which Paul refers in verse 13 are to be linked with Luke's record in Acts 28:30, "And Paul dwelt two whole years in his own hired house." The place, then, would be Rome. The form of his captivity would thus be neither the severest (in a cell or dungeon) nor the mildest (something roughly equivalent to being "out on bail") that Rome practiced. It was the middle form, in which the prisoner would have something to say about his abode but, wherever, would have to submit to being guarded day and night by the military.

II. EXPOSITORY MEANING

1:13. "My bonds in Christ are manifest" is better rendered in most of our newer translations; in the Revised Standard Version for example: "it has become known . . . that my imprisonment is for Christ." What is exhibited is not the bonds but the *reason* for the bonds. Similarly "palace" is better translated as in the Revised Standard Version, "the whole praetorian guard." Praetorian" is in fact an Anglicized form of the Greek word. It may be used to describe either a place or a collection of people. When used in reference to a place, the meaning varied from (1) a general's field headquarters to (2) the residence of an important official, to (3) the house or villa of an influential person. When used in reference to people, its definition was quite specific. It meant the soldiers of the Imperial Guard. (In rare instances it is said to have meant the barracks in which they were quartered.) Says Marvin Vincent, in the *International Critical Commentary*, "they were ten thousand in number, picked men, originally of Italian birth, but drawn later from Macedonia, Noricum and Spain. They were originally instituted by Augustus, who stationed three of their cohorts in Rome, and dispersed the others in the adjacent towns." Day after day, week after week, soldiers from this crack regiment would be assigned for guard duty in Paul's house.

1:14. The phrase "of the Lord" may be taken to modify "confident" rather than "brethren." The grammatical construction of the sentence permits it, and Vincent, for example, feels that the sense is better served by it: "By Paul's bonds the brethren have had their *confidence in the Lord* strengthened" (italics ours).

1:15. "Some indeed preach Christ even of envy and strife." They are further described in verse 16 as those who "preach Christ of contention, not sincerely." Who are they? This is what Simcox calls "the first baffling note in the Letter." It has given rise to what Vincent labels "much wearisome discussion." Strictly speaking, the problem is not exegetical. There is no serious dispute about the meaning of the words that Paul uses. There is no dispute about the purity of the Greek text. The difference of interpretation arises from the question: To whom is Paul referring? Unbelievers (who "talked up" the gospel only that they might inflame the hatred of Paul's foes)? So Chrysostom. Jews (who discussed the gospel only in order to refute and discredit)? So Grotius. Judaizing Christians (mixing Law and Grace)? So Bengel, Lightfoot, Meyer, Beet, and others. Or were they what we call today "evangelical Christians" who were "personally jealous of the apostle, and sought to undermine his influence"? So Vincent, Finlayson, Barclay, and presumably Moule. "As a matter of fact," says Robertson, "it is quite likely that all of these elements enter into the situation, for Paul expressly says that these men proclaimed Christ from mixed motives, 'not sincerely.' "

1:19. "This shall turn to my salvation." "Salvation," not in the sense of physical deliverance, and certainly not in the sense of securing eternal life or God's reconciling favor; but, rather, as related to the apostle's total well-being in the ordering of the divine providence. "The supply of the Spirit of Jesus Christ." Some scholars take it subjectively (the giving of the Spirit Himself), others objectively (that which the Holy Spirit gives in aid and support). Being truly trinitarian, Paul does not hesitate to identify the Holy Spirit with Christ even as he does with God.

1:20. "My earnest expectation and my hope." "Earnest expectation" is a single picturesque word in the Greek. It means, literally, to *turn away the head.* One shuts other subjects from the field of one's vision in order to concentrate on the object of interest and desire. If a distinction is to be drawn between the "expectation" and the "hope," perhaps it is that the former indicates the outer, or more visible, aspect of this intentness, while the latter signifies the inner attitude. The New English Bible tries to capture the substance of both words in the translation "I passionately hope."

"That in nothing I shall be ashamed." That is, he is confident that he will never find himself in the position of a deluded herald, a misguided enthusiast whose faith and witness have been shown to be false.

"With all boldness." It is especially the courage of utterance, or in today's familiar phrase, "freedom of speech," on which Lightfoot makes the comment that "the right of free speech is the badge, the privilege, of the servant of Christ."

"Christ shall be magnified in my body." The unfailing courage of witness was to be Paul's; the glory was to be Christ's And this was to be the case whether the apostle lived or died.

1:22. "If I live in the flesh, this is the fruit of my labor." The construction in the Greek is so broken as to permit a variety of renderings. Professor Robertson's reconstruction is noteworthy: "But if life in the flesh (be my lot), this means for me fruit of work." That is to say, Living on in the body will afford me more opportunity for work and hence for fruit.

"I wot not." The archaic form is replaced by the simple "I cannot tell" of the Revised Standard Version and the New English Bible.

1:23. "Having a desire to depart." Literally, *to break up, to unloose* — used nautically of freeing a ship from its moorings or militarily of breaking up a camp, the latter form of the metaphor being much more congenial to Paul's mind.

1:27. "Let your conversation be as becometh the gospel." Literally, as Moule suggests, "live your citizen-life." As Roman citizens, of whom Paul was one and of whom many could be found in Philippi, seek to live responsibly according to the order of the empire, so Christians are to order their lives in such a manner as to bear witness to their higher citizenship in the Kingdom of Christ (cf. 3:20).

1:28. "Which is to them an evident token of perdition, but to you of salvation." Moule's expository amplification is useful: "Such calm united courage is to them an evidence, a sure token, an omen, of the perdition that awaits the obstinate foes of holiness, but to you of the salvation which awaits Christ's faithful witnesses."

1:29. "Having the same conflict." The Greek word for "conflict" has entered our English language in the form of "agony." Its original reference was to a contest in the arena. It signifies, by extension, any severe struggle, internal or external. The Philippians must know that their conflict with the enemies of the gospel is essentially the same as that which they witnessed within their own city when Paul was flogged and jailed, and as that in which he is now involved in Rome.

III. DOCTRINAL VALUE. While this portion of the Letter is primarily autobiographical, its theological implications emerge suggestively as follows: (1) the doctrine of Providence (vv. 12, 29), (2) the doctrine of Prayer (v. 19), (3) the doctrine of the Holy Spirit (v. 19), (4) the doctrine of the Christian's mystical union with Christ (v. 21), and (5) the doctrine of Future Things (v. 23).

IV. PRACTICAL AIM. To nourish in fellow Christians the unshakable conviction that suffering is part of the scheme of life and that Christian victory, far from consisting in exemption from it, consists in triumphing over it by turning it to the greater honor of Christ and the wider extension of His Kingdom.

V. HOMILETICAL FORM

Theme: "When Difficulties Become Doors."

Introduction: Not what happens to us, but the way we react to what happens — this is crucial to the Christian management of life. From his pillow of piercing pain Ralph Erskine testified, "I have known more of God since I came to this bed than through all my life." It is faith's incredible way of grasping the nettle and extracting nectar from it. Not the tragic event, but the turning of the event into something other than tragic — this is the victory.

It was Paul's. It may be ours.

But to speak of faith in some broad and airy way is not enough. With Paul faith is always linked with an amazing proclamation that he keeps calling the gospel and with this amazing Person that he has come to know as Jesus Christ. He may speak now of one and now the other, but in each case the one implies the other. Both doctrinally and dynamically, they are forever met together.

Listen to this man whose free spirit leaps out from his fettered body as he writes to his friends in Philippi: "your fellowship in the gospel" — it means more to me than I can possibly tell; "the furtherance of the gospel" — that is the outcome of my imprisonment; "the defense of the gospel" — this is my occupation, and everybody who knows me knows it; "the faith of the gospel" — this is the scheme of reality in which I want all of my Christian friends to stand.

All this ardent accent on the gospel in what we call the first chapter of his letter!

Looking at Paul, this gospel-saturated man who is now Caesar's captive, we think, first of all, of —

A. *The Difficulties That Advance the Gospel*

Carroll Simcox has done a translation of Philippians in which verse 12 reads: "I want you to know, brethren, that these things that have happened to me serve for the advancement of the gospel." Liabilities have been converted into assets. Frustrations have been transformed into fulfillments. The very troubles that might have stopped the gospel have been captured and made to serve the gospel.

What are these difficulties?

Physical limitations, for one thing. This Knight of the Cross — he of the burning heart and the long, long trail — where is he now? Week after week, month after month, no journey made, no sea crossed, no highway travelled, no new city entered. Instead, the monotony of this custody in which he was being held by the police power of Rome!

Yet this physical confinement was providing Paul with the opportunity to communicate the Good News in places where normally he would have had no access. We shall say more about this in a moment.

Physical handicap can be a baffling and embittering frustration or it can be turned into an exciting fulfillment at levels of life on which we have rarely, if ever, moved. Years ago I read about a professor in Union Theological Seminary, Richmond, Virginia, who one day, while lecturing, quoted Romans 8:28. In discussion one of his students said, "But, professor, you don't believe that 'all things work together for good' — all the pain and suffering and misery — do you?" His reply was, "The things in themselves may not be good, but you can make them work together for good." Before that day's sun went down his wife was killed in an automobile accident, and he was injured in a way that left him a cripple. When the president of the seminary called on him, he said, "Tell my students that Romans 8:28 still holds good!" Before a year had passed death kissed him into the heavenly Father's nearer presence. They inscribed Romans 8:28 on his tomb. One man, who rose to be one of the South's most eminent preachers, testified that repeatedly he visited this tomb and prayerfully drank in the spirit of that dauntless

professor. Crippled, he conquered. Physically deprived, he
became more spiritually released and creative than ever.

Another difficulty that Paul found it possible to harness
in the service of the gospel was *social humiliation*. Was this
man a prisoner? Then he must endure the stigma that would
be stamped on his name. In verse 13 where the Authorized
Version reads "my bonds" the New English Bible reads "my
imprisonment."

Yet this indignity was in two ways turned to the gospel's
advantage: it gave the gospel a new sphere in which to work
and it gave to the friends of the gospel in Rome a new
strength in which to testify. As for the first effect, it is ad-
mirably brought out in the Phillips rendering of verse 13:
"my imprisonment means a personal witness for Christ before the Palace guards, not to mention others who come and
go." Paul had testified to the Good News of Jesus before the
Jews of Rome, but how was he to reach into the high, smug
ranks of these picked imperial guardsmen? The answer, as
it turned out, was a humiliating one: become a prisoner
under them.

Day and night a soldier was at his side: first one and then
another, as each day passed, and the days became weeks, and
the weeks became months. When it began, Paul was to them
just another criminal, or, if not that, just another political
prisoner. They soon found that, as we say, they "had another
guess coming." Why was this man in irons? Because of what
he believed and taught about Jesus. Who was Jesus? Who
are these Christians? What are they trying to do? Are they
a threat to Caesar? to law and order? to the gods? So the
Christian message got to be known in circles where Caesar,
certainly, never suspected that it would make an impression.
We have no proof that Paul ever made a personal appearance in the emperor's palace. All we know is that there were
"saints" in "Caesar's household" (4:22). Perhaps it was a
member of the praetorium who, convinced or curious, converted or just aroused, carried the exciting message.

Thus, Paul's difficulty, which looked like a thwarting wall,
became an open door. Adversity was turned to advantage.

In 17th century England George Fox and the Quakers were making their witness. Hundreds were being converted. The complacency of "established" religion was being stabbed awake by the irresistable weapons of Christian sincerity and vitality. While preaching at the Castle of Carlisle in the north of England, Fox was arrested on charges of blasphemy and, after trial, was thrown into a filthy dungeon already overrun with vermin and criminals. Scarcely a friend who came to see him was allowed even a glimpse of him. Some who tried to bring him food were beaten back by the under-jailer's club. A hundred and fifty miles away, sixteen-year-old James Parnell, a cripple endowed with a brilliant mind, heard about Fox's plight, walked the long miles, managed to get inside the prison, was never the same again. Says Walter Williams, in his volume on Quaker history, "After he and George Fox spent some time in fellowship together, the lad left Carlisle dungeon with heart aflame, and gave the rest of his life to Christ and the Friends Movement." While "the rest of his life" was not long — less than three years — it was penetratingly influential through the literary efforts that he dedicated to the spiritual awakening and renewal of the church.

Difficulty is *not* all darkness. Eyes there must be for the points of light that appear in the blackness.

Paul's imprisonment, moreover, was turned to advantage among the Christians in Rome. Their courage in witness, he tells the Philippians, has been shored up: they are "much more bold to speak the word without fear" (v. 14). True, some of them are doing their preaching from motives less than noble, but even that, says the apostle, does not prevent his extracting some satisfaction from it. After all, Christ *is* being proclaimed. Comrades who have been silent are vocal for Christ. Brothers who have been timid are outspoken. Dread of trouble has given way to delight in testimony. "I therein do rejoice; yea, and will rejoice!" (v. 18).

> "Then let me keep my moment, gracious Lord;
>   Unhinged from men and bound alone to Thee.
>   Enactments of Thy glory now afford,

Let this small place Thine own arena be.
And at the striking of the hour
Pour out Thy grace and show Thy power."[1]

From the difficulties that advance the gospel let us move on to think of —

B. *The Dilemmas That Arise from the Gospel*

"Dilemma" indeed is the very word that Weymouth uses in his translation of verse 23: "I am in a dilemma, my earnest desire being to depart and be with Christ, for that is far, far better. But for your sakes it is more important that I should still remain in the body." "Dilemma" is Moffatt's word, too.

Let us be sure that we understand precisely what is in Paul's mind when he speaks of this delicate balancing of alternatives. It is not, strictly speaking, the "life or death" dilemma. In grim circumstances and low moods many a person has asked desperately, "Which is better, to be dead or alive?" This was neither the apostle's feeling nor his problem.

Nor is it the "existence or non-existence" dilemma. In Hamlet's pathetic self-querying he sighs, "To be, or not to be, that is the question." But it is not! That is only the *fancied* question. Once we *are,* we shall never cease to *be.* Yet there are times, especially when life itself seems to make no sense, when despair of meaning whelms the mind, when sheer emptiness stares at us from all four walls — times when the longing for annihilation vies with the desire for being. Yet this tragic tension stands poles apart from the problem on which Paul opens his heart to the Philippians.

What, then, was it?

Since we made mention of Hamlet, we may find him useful in pointing up sharply the character of Paul's momentary indecision. Hamlet represents any man who is obsessed by the evils and complications of life. Our apostle, on the other hand, represents the Christian man who is convinced of, and obsessed by, the goodness, the worthwhileness, the richness, of life. Your Hamlets, brought to extremity, try to assess the

---

[1] Geoffrey Bull, *God Holds the Key* (Chicago: Moody Press) p. 29.

troubles of life, from which death (in their view) would free them, against the terror of death, from which life shields them. But your Pauls, moved by utterly different considerations, are not found trying to weigh two sets of bitters against one another, but two sets of sweets. Life here, this side of death, is good; life there, on the other side of death, is better.

Both terms of the dilemma, moreover, have their secret and their center in Christ.

Which, therefore, to choose?

Closely linked with this problem is a second: the dilemma in which the apostle weighs happiness for himself against helpfulness for his brethren. Here we have the tension between verse 24 (the last part) and verse 25. "To be with Christ," says Paul, is "far better" for me. "Nevertheless to abide in the flesh is more needful for you." "For your sake there is greater need for me to stay on in the body" is the way the New English Bible puts it.

In delightful and discerning comment on this verse J. H. Jowett once wrote: "To have helped somebody a few steps along the heavenly road, to have infused a little more holy courage into their spirits, to have given a more exuberant swing to their stride — these services abundantly justify a delay in the journey, and will assure for us a more glorious welcome in our Father's house."

Actually, this summons of human need, this invitation to helpfulness, becomes the key that unlocks the dilemma in both of its forms: the apostle will let his own bliss stand aside and wait while the blessing of others goes forward.

Thus the dilemmas that arise from the gospel, unlike those that grow out of human selfishness and striving, do not tear us to bits, leaving us with nerves frazzled, the will paralyzed, the health destroyed. If we ask why, the answer, surely, lies in the simple declaration that Paul makes in verse 21: "For to me to live is Christ." "The essence of our life . . . the model of our life . . . the aim of our life . . . the solace of our life . . . the reward of our life" — it is all there, as F. B. Meyer rightly insists, in Him! Because life in Him is everything, death is

incidental. "Safe shall be my going," sang Rupert Brooke,
> "Secret armed against all death's endeavor;
> Safe though all safety's lost; safe where men fall;
> And if these poor limbs die, safest of all."

Ah, yes, difficulties and dilemmas there must be in lives we call Christian. It were folly to deny it. What we must never forget, however, is that when the Christian man whose spirit has been joined to Christ confronts them, they turn out to be, not a blind alley, not a frustrating road to nowhere, but a beckoning portal and a luring path, along which are set the unquenchable lights of hope.

Think, therefore, and finally, of —

C. The Dauntlessness That Attends the Gospel

The firm fiber of our faith is underscored in each of the last four verses of the chapter:

"Stand fast," cries the apostle in verse 27.

"And in nothing terrified by your adversaries," is the bracing summons of verse 28.

"Unto you it is given in the behalf of Christ ... to suffer for his sake," is the startling turn of thought found in verse 29.

While verse 30 reminds us that "the same conflict" the same essential struggle of light and darkness, which we have seen in Paul's life, must be fought out in our own.

The undaunted Christian is the Christian who knows the value of sheer *fidelity*. "Let me know that you are standing firm" (v. 27) is the way the New English Bible reads. "The world," says one of our living commentators, "is full of Christians on the retreat." A thousand pities!

The undaunted Christian is the Christian who, relying upon Christ, believes in his *invincibility*. "Meeting your opponents without so much as a tremor" (v. 28, NEB). "Not caring two straws for your enemies," is the vivid rendering of Phillips. No panic! Just calm, unshatterable confidence in the Victor "whose we are and whom we serve!"

The undaunted Christian is the Christian who lives with an awareness of his *accountability*. Simcox and others trans-

late verse 29: "For to you is given the privilege not simply
of believing in Christ but of suffering for him." Suffering is
a trust and a privilege — how strangely that falls on the ears
of a generation that flees discomfort with swifter feet than
it flees depravity! Nor dare we Christians forget that, as our
Lord put it, "unto whomsoever much is given, of him shall
be much required" (Luke 12:48). Morbidly to seek suffering
is foolish and neurotic. Nevertheless, when it comes, it is the
business of God's man to take hold of it, use it, make it
yield up "the treasures of darkness" it holds; and then, in
the end, be ready to give an account of his stewardship.

The undaunted Christian, moreover, is the Christian who
in trouble's ceaseless battle is full of *sympathy*. I use the
word sympathy now in its more precise meaning of *fellow-
feeling*. It is both the capability and the action of identifying
ourselves with others. This is well brought out by the New
English Bible rendering of verse 30: "You and I are engaged
in the same contest; you saw me in it once, and, as you hear,
I am in it still." Isolation — sometimes physical and psychological, sometimes psychological only — tends to generate
self-pity; and self-pity, any day in the week, is the death of
courage.

"We are in this fight together," cries Paul. "Let us carry
on, mutually aware of human frailties and insufficiencies,
mutually confident of our boundless resources in the vic-
torious Lord we have and hold in common."

Here then is Paul the undaunted pleading for dauntless-
ness in the life of his Christian comrades. No one ever had
a better right to make such a plea. In *Apostle Extraordinary*,
one of the latest of the many books on the life and character
of Paul, R. E. O. White lays it down, with full justification, that "Nothing could frighten Paul's dauntless soul, or
intimidate his judgment. As the whole Christian cause of
Church *versus* State moved to its climax of pressure and
peril, the Church could have found no stauncher champion
in whom the conflict might be focused, or by whom the
steadfastness and courage of all Christian hearts could be
nourished and inspired."

It is this man who is stubbornly certain that no matter what happens to give pause or pain to the friends of Jesus Christ, the gospel in which they put their trust will be advanced, not retarded. Far from being frustrated, it will be furthered.

> "Yea, thro' life, death, thro' sorrow and thro' sinning
> He shall suffice me, for He hath sufficed;
> Christ is the end, for Christ was the beginning,
> Christ is the beginning, for the end is Christ."

Always, come harrowing or horror, Christ is the way through!

Philippians 2

ARE WE CHRIST-MINDED?

2:5. "*Let this mind be in you, which was also in Christ Jesus.*"

I. HISTORICAL SETTING. The assembly of believers at Philippi was flawed at just one point: it was threatened with factions and dissensions. A hint of this comes through in 1:27, where Paul urges: "stand fast in one spirit." The hint is much stronger at the beginning of Chapter 2: "be like-minded . . . of one accord, of one mind. Let nothing be done through strife or vainglory" (vv. 2, 3). The cure for this, Paul argues, is the grace of humility, "lowliness of mind" (v. 3); and the secret of humility lies in our being possessed by "the mind of Christ."

II. EXPOSITORY MEANING
2:1. The "if," which in the Authorized Version occurs four times in verse 1, indicates not doubt but certainty. It is used rhetorically to "get a grip on their attention," as Robertson puts it. "Bowels and mercies" becomes "affection and sympathy" in the Revised Standard Version. We use the organ of the heart when we want an image-identification for tender feelings. The ancients, on the other hand, saw nothing strange in using the viscera for the same purpose. The two words that Paul uses speak first of the seat of compassion and then of the compassion itself.

2:3. Rather than "strife" (AV) or "selfishness" (RSV), many expositors prefer some such rendering as "a party spirit." Cliquishness and factiousness appear clearly to be in the apostle's mind. "Lowliness of mind," which is one word in the Greek, is a coinage from the mint of the gospel. The first half, without the second, occurs in classical Greek, but is used in the sense of *meanness* or *abjectness*. Paul compounds it with a word that suggests something roughly analogous to our common expression, "frame of mind." What comes to birth is that modesty of self-assessment which is learned at the Saviour's feet.

2:4. "Also" must not be overlooked. It gives perspective and balance to what Paul is urging. What is forbidden is the fixing of one's eye on one's own interests to the exclusion of the interests of others. This is virtually the way Professor Robertson phrases his discerning insight into this sentence.

2:5. The Revised Standard Version alters the reading of the Authorized Version so as to read "Have this mind among yourselves." Vincent, long antedating the Revised Standard Version, argues against this reading. "In you" seems best. The "in" is collective as well as personal. Literally, "Be having this disposition or spirit in yourselves which was in Christ."

2:6. "Form" indicates not *material shape* but *essential nature*. Christ's eternal and inherently rightful status is that of deity. "Robbery" is a mystifying translation of a word that is difficult to render into English without awkwardness. Technically, it indicates a *process* of plunder, whereas context indicates that Paul has in mind an *object* of plunder. Moule's amplification is supportable and helpful: He "reckoned it no plunderer's prize to be on an equality with God." Had He regarded it as being such a prize, he would have greedily clung to it, mindful of none but Himself.

2:7. "Made himself of no reputation" is well rendered in the Revised Standard Version, "emptied himself."

"The form of a servant" means that the essential nature of the bond-servant (not having any rights of one's own but submitting, rather, to the authority of another) was conjoined with the essential nature of deity in the one person, Jesus Christ.

"Made in the likeness of men" is a clause requiring careful exegesis. The "likeness" was real; it was not a mask, making of Jesus a phantom man. Yet the identity with humanity, for all its genuineness, was restricted in the sense that His humanity fell short of expressing the whole of His selfhood. He who assumed the "likeness of men" retained "the form of God" while so doing. Out of the verb-form translated "was made" (literally, "having become") Barclay attempts to erect a theory of *temporariness* in respect of the humanity of Christ. "The manhood of Jesus," he asserts, "was not permanent; He became man, but only for a time. . . . His manhood was utterly real, but it was something which passed." Theologically, it would appear to be a case of Homer nodding. Scholars such as Ellicott and Robertson echo the witness of the church universal that our Lord's "humanity was permanently added to His divinity. He is the Son of man now as well as the Son of God which He was before" (so Robertson).

2:8. "Revealed in human shape" is the New English Bible translation of the phrase which the Authorized Version renders "being found in fashion as a man." The Greek word for "fashion" is nicely designed to set out the difference between *essential nature* and *circumstantial appearance*. His being in the "form of God" was a veiled reality, but His looking like a man — eating, drinking, walking, talking — was something perfectly obvious to those who met Him. It was while He was in this state of manifest humanity that He further humbled Himself in that supremely self-effacing act of obedience to the Father's sovereign will which took Him to the cross.

2:9. "Wherefore" may be taken as simple *consequence* or as a *reward*. Calvin protests against the latter. Vincent regards the protest as needless, agreeing with Meyer that in any event "Christ's saying in Matthew 28:12 was gloriously fulfilled in His own case."

"Highly exalted" is from a Greek compound of Paul's which can mean (1) exalted *more than before* or (2) simply exalted in *superlative degree*. If the former, it raises the question of *when*: before the exaltation took place (in which case the assertion would seem to be too obvious) or before the self-emptying occurred? Some expositors see here an affirmation that there attaches to the "last Adam, the Lord from heaven," a glory that transcends the glory of the pre-incarnate Son of God. Most, however, (and this applies to translators as well as exegetes) would appear to agree with Vincent that the force of Paul's word "is not 'more than before,' nor 'above His previous state of humiliation,' but 'in superlative measure.' " "A name which is above every name" is taken to mean: (1) "Jesus" (for which Maclaren pleads movingly), (2) "Jesus Christ" (so Vincent), (3) "Lord" (what to the Hebrews was the ineffable name *Jehovah*), or (4) "dignity," "majesty," "reputation" (a view argued by Lightfoot).

2:10. "At the name" is better rendered, as in later versions, "in the name." The name is not a magical title; it is a meaningful disclosure: the Person comes through in His name.

"Every knee" introduces the fulfillment of Isaiah 45:23, which Paul pictorially interprets as, in Moule's language, "all created existence, in its heights and depths; spirits, men, and every other creature; all bowing, each in their way, to the *imperium* of the exalted Jesus."

2:11. "Confess" is taken by some to mean simply to "declare openly"; by others (Lightfoot, for example) it is held to mean "confess with thanksgiving."

"Jesus Christ is Lord" is believed by many scholars to be an authentic echo of the earliest Christian creed. Is it the *fact* that Christ is Lord that is "to the glory of God the Father," or is it the *confession* of the fact? Probably the latter.

2:12. "Wherefore" points up the Christian logic, so to speak, lying behind all that the apostle has been saying thus far in the chapter: the way to real fulfillment, excellence, and honor is not that of personal feuding or factional striving but of self-effacing, as is demonstrated so signally and sublimely in the case of our Lord.

"Work out your own salvation." What is yours as a free gift is yours also as a trust; therefore carry out its high and holy meanings consistently.

"With fear and trembling" is a reading retained by several later versions. Moffatt alters it to read "with reverence and trembling," while Vincent translates it "with conscientious caution and self-distrust." A deeply sensitive filial regard combined with a wholesome shrinking back from the peril of failure — this is the becoming mood for which Paul pleads. One of these perils, to which some members of the assembly had fallen victim, was that of high-headedness resulting in dissension. Be afraid of all haughtiness or pettiness that ruptures the fellowship!

2:13. "God which worketh in you" is the enabling correlative of your duty to "work out." The out-working of Christian salvation may be the believer's responsibility but it is quite impossible without the in-working of God's energy. Grace and free-will, for all their interlocking mystery, are not ultimately contradictory.

2:14. "Murmurings." The Greek is onomatopoetic, perhaps more nearly approximated by the English word "grumblings."

"Disputings" is used in a bad sense: ill-natured controversies.

2:15. Three descriptive terms that we cannot afford to misread and which we dare not explain away: "blameless," "harmless," "without rebuke." Before the world — "blameless"; in themselves (through union with Christ) — "harmless," or, better, *unalloyed, uncorrupted;* under the eye of God — "without rebuke," irreproachable. Barclay's whole paragraph of exegesis is excellent.

2:16. "Holding forth." What is suggested is the *sharing of a gift;* or, "holding fast," in which case what is suggested is the preserving of a treasure. The Revised Standard Version uses the latter, although the Authorized Version seems best.

"The word of life" is the gospel, which, as Vincent puts it, "has in itself a principle as well as a message of life."

"In the day of Christ," meaning against, or *in view of, the day of judgment and rewards.*

"Labored." The Greek is strong, meaning *exhausting toil.*

2:17. "Offered upon the sacrifice" is a picture phrase, drawn from the pagan practice of pouring a libation upon the sacrifice to the gods. A paraphrase of the verse might be: "You are offering to God your faith in Christ. So intense is my desire that this faith of yours shall bear the fruit of light and witness which God intends for it that if I die in carrying out my service to you, I shall gladly regard my poured out life as the sacrifice that crowns your offering of faith."

2:20. "Likeminded." Literally, of *equal soul,* meaning that there is no one here with me who measures up to Timothy in respect of oneness with me in anxious concern about you.

"Naturally." Literally, by *birth relation,* signifying *genuineness.*

2:21. "For all seek their own" is a stricture so severe that Vincent may be right in holding that "without more information a satisfactory explanation seems impossible." Augustine and Anselm took this to mean that Paul's companions in Rome were mercenaries. Could this be true of Luke? Or was Luke away when Paul wrote this?

2:25. "Messenger," from the Greek word for *apostle.* J. B. Phillips likes to translate it "special messenger."

"Ministered" is a noun in the Greek, meaning one who performs a service or ministry. Our English word "liturgy" is derived from this term. Among the Greeks a *liturgon* was a public-spirited citizen who out of his own resources rendered some conspicuous service to the community. Thus it is a word held in high honor that Paul here appropriates and applies to Epaphroditus.

2:28. "I sent." The tense used here, and in verse 25 as well, is an epistolary aorist, whose force is, in our idiom, "I send."

2:29. "Hold such in reputation" is well rendered in the Revised Standard Version "honor such men."

2:30. "Not regarding his life" is a phrase drawn — and redeemed — from the world of gambling. Epaphroditus risked his life, in reckless disregard of his own safety.

"To supply your lack of service toward me" is well done in the New English Bible: "To render me the service you could not give."

III. DOCTRINAL VALUE. Although, as Lightfoot observes, this Epistle is "the least dogmatic of the apostle's letters," it contains one of the sublimest — perhaps *the* sublimest — passages in the New Testament on the person and work of Jesus Christ. It is in verses 5-11 of this chapter. True, it appears not by way of deliberate theological intention, and least of all by way of theological argument, but rather by way of enforcing and superbly illustrating the practical counsel to live *humbly* and therefore *harmoniously*.

True, also, that the structure of the passage is poetic and hymn-like, not formally instructional or dogmatic.

What Paul here *assumes* to be apostolic faith is every bit as meaningful as if this were a predetermined attempt to declare the primitive church's dogma regarding the unique person and the saving work of Christ. Caffin, in *The Pulpit Commentary* (volume on Philippians and Colossians), puts the matter lucidly: "The great doctrinal passage in the second chapter asserts most of the distinctive articles of the Christian creed. St. Paul insists upon the divinity of Christ, His pre-existence, His equality with God the Father, His incarnation, His perfect humanity, His precious death upon the cross, His glorious exaltation." This the faith which the church exultantly *sings*.

IV. PRACTICAL AIM. It is stated negatively in the first part of verse 3: "Let nothing be done through strife or vainglory"; and positively in the last part: "in lowliness of mind let each esteem other better than themselves." Take note of this: just where doctrine is being held soundly and life in Christ is being expressed vigorously is where dissension was in the bud and threatening to burst into an evil flowering. It is in this context that, as Moule puts it, Paul plies the Philippians "with every loving argument for the unity of love, ranging from the plea of attachment to himself up to the supreme plea of 'the mind that was in Christ Jesus' when He came down from heaven."

V. HOMILETICAL FORM
    Theme: "Are We Christ-Minded?"

Introduction: "I am a Christian," said a Scotsman of an earlier generation, "I am a Christian because the Reverend Marcus Dods is a Christian. Talk about the evidences of Christianity, Dods is it!" If the Apostle Paul could have heard that simple, glowing testimony, he would have smiled. His smile would be his way of saying, "That's what I told the Philippians: that everyone of them was meant to be a walking proof of Jesus Christ, so possessed by His spirit that they could reproduce it, so given over to His disposition that they could convey its self-effacing attractiveness wherever they went."

See now how Paul takes this humblemindedness of the Master, holds it up to the light, and asks us to examine it.

What do we see?

A. For one thing, we see that it is the mind of *self-emptying*. Listen to Weymouth's translation: "From the beginning He had the nature of God. Yet He did not regard equality with God as something at which He should grasp. Nay, He stripped Himself of His glory" (vv. 6, 7). "He emptied Himself," is a literal putting of the Greek. Tennyson's couplet is recalled:

"The Lord of all things made Himself
Naked of glory for His mortal change."

Many years ago, when the Duke of Windsor was the Prince of Wales, he one day left Buckingham Palace, journeyed west into the coal mining country, put on a miner's cap, and went down into the dingy tunnels to see for himself the conditions in which men toiled in a difficult and dangerous branch of British industry. As a member of the royal family he was as much a prince in the coal mine as he was when he lived in the palace in London. But, while his essential equality with royalty was unchanged, there was no longer an equality of *experience*. He had consented to enter into experiences that never came to him amid the elegances and immunities of the palace.

So when the eternal Son of God became the Jesus of history, when "the word was made flesh," as John puts it, He did not empty Himself of His essential deity. What He obviously did was to strip Himself of the heavenly majesty associated with His deity. Emily Elliott's Homely hymn — and I use the word "homely" in its British, complimentary sense — says it memorably:

> "Thou didst leave Thy throne and Thy kingly crown,
>   When Thou camest to earth for me;
>   But in Bethlehem's home there was found no room
>   For Thy holy nativity.
>
> "Heaven's arches rang when the angels sang,
>   Proclaiming Thy royal degree,
>   But in lowly birth didst Thou come to earth,
>   And in great humility."

We must try to see now the practical target at which Paul is thrusting as he shows us this humblemindedness at its purest and best — in Jesus. The immediate need of the Philippian church is a new sense of Christian unity. The bond of brotherliness has not been broken. It has, however, been threatened. Hence the ardor of Paul's appeal: "stand fast in one spirit, with one mind striving together for the faith of the gospel" (1:27).

There are two mischievous things, the apostle points out, which will interfere with, and eventually destroy, this unity. One is brought forward in verse 3, the other in verse 4. "Do nothing from selfishness or conceit" (RSV). Here is the *self-importance* which insists that others shall bend to its interest. Then follows: "Let each of you look not only to his own interests, but also to the interests of others" (RSV). Here, by implication, is the *self-absorption* that makes it impossible to give the interests of others a consideration which at least equals the consideration it gives to its own interests.

Our Lord, in His self-emptying, provides us with a perfect example of one who completely sidestepped both of these destructive evils. If He had looked only "to his own interests," He would have held fast to his heavenly mode of existence in which there was the full recognition of his co-equality with God. It would not have been "robbery." It would not have been unseemly. This honor was His by eternal right.

Nonetheless, He let it go. He refused to insist on it. He turned His back on it. An unredeemed world needed Him. When there was no "arm to save" and no "eye to pity,"

"He saw and, Oh, amazing love,
He flew to our relief."

Such was the self-foregoing, the self-emptying, of Christ which, in inner principle, is to become operative in us as we surrender ourselves to His "mind."

B. Looked at from another angle, the mind of Christ is the mind of *service:* "He took upon him the form of a servant" (v. 7).

"As Christ possessed the real attributes of deity," says Robertson, "so He took upon Himself the real attributes of servantship." Only let us be clear that it was not by abandoning the divine Sonship that He assumed the human servantship. It was by uniting the two in a living personal synthesis.

In Western culture "service" is a verbal coinage that has been debased. It has been pretty thoroughly commercialized. An international club of business men has for its motto, "Service Above Self." Admittedly, the motto means more to some members than to others. Still, it is hard to escape the feeling that the "service" angle has a hard time to climb out on top of the "self" angle.

What is easy for us to overlook is the difference between rendering service and being a servant. "It is damnably easy," exclaims D. T. Niles of Ceylon, "to dole out service; it is not so easy to be a servant."

When Jesus finished washing the disciples' feet, He did not say, "I want you to render service." He said, in effect, "I want you to be servants." What He did in fact say was: "The *servant* is not greater than his lord" (John 13:16). The slave is not to think himself better or more elevated than his master. On the contrary, the Christian disciple is to take the role of a servant in the conviction that if his Lord took it before him, then even a slave's part can be counted an affair of honor.

Listen to this from a missionary who has spent long years

in India, writing about the kind of young missionary who will be effective as a co-worker in the Indian churches today:

"He must not be an individualist or, in the old sense, a pioneer. He must come in the spirit of saying to the Indian Church, 'What do you want me to do?' rather than 'Here is something that I want to do for you; will you let me do it?' He must be ready always to take second place and often see Indians less qualified than himself set above him; but he must not refuse office and responsibility when it comes to him at the call of the Indian Church. He must come for life and not in the spirit of a trial marriage, and that in spite of the fact that political conditions might at some time make life service impossible."

If that description adds up to anything at all, it adds up to a re-enactment of the washing of the disciples' feet. It is the "mind of Christ" molded into "the form of a servant." I say this without necessarily endorsing the rigor of every sentence in the quotation.

God the sovereign has become, in Christ, God the servant; and He has made the Son of His love to rule over a kingdom of servants.

C. We move on to a third facet of the Christly mind: it is the mind of *sympathy.* "He was made," says Paul, "in the likeness of men." The word "form" is not used now, since Christ's voluntary disengagement from the divine glory in order to assume the nature of a "servant" has already been established. Here it is asserted that in becoming servant He became genuinely human. Not human *only,* but human *truly!*

Thus the Son of God identifies Himself with the sons of men. This is the deeper meaning of "sympathy." We have narrowed the word to mean tears at a funeral or a card of condolence dropped into the mail box.

In the full strength and stature of its significance it means to "feel with," which is even more than to "feel for." Who can say that the priest and Levite did not in some measure *feel for* the man who had been felled by robbers? But it was the Samaritan who demonstrated the ability *to feel with.* He identified himself with the roadside victim, put himself,

with sensitive imagination, in his place. Out from that identification flowed action: first aid given, wounds bound up, the
hospitality of a wayside inn assured, full recovery promised.

The writer to the letter to the Hebrews seizes this idea,
holds it up for us, and asks us to see it perfectly embodied
in Jesus: "For verily he took not on him the nature of
angels; but he took on him the seed of Abraham. Wherefore
in all things it behooved him to be made like unto his
brethren" — and now note the reason: "that he might be a
merciful and faithful high priest in things pertaining to
God, to make reconciliation for the sins of the people. For
in that he himself hath suffered being tempted, he is able to
succor them that are tempted" (2:16-18).

Unless this mind of sympathetic identification is in us, our
love will be sentimental, our vision misty, and our service
perfunctory. It was after Ezekiel could say of the captives
down by the Chebar, "I sat where they sat" (3:15) that he
was able to minister to them from within their situation of
need. It was when Dan Crawford learned what "Thinking
Black" really meant that he was enabled to reach the African
heart.

D. Christmindedness includes, also, the mind of *submission*.
"He humbled himself," is Paul's way of putting it, "and became obedient unto death" (v. 8). Phillips has it, "he
humbled Himself by living a life of utter obedience."

It is part of the Christian understanding of the earthly,
human life of the Son of God that He put Himself under
the discipline of the Father's will. He thus made Himself
an example of that submissive loyalty that emphatically
witnesses, "I came down from heaven, not to do mine own
will, but the will of him that sent me" (John 6:38).

The modern mind, for all its boasting, is often blind and
bull-headed. It mistakes license for liberty and fetterlessness
for freedom. It is an obscene mind, in the precise meaning of
that word: it is *out of place*. Chesterton's comment is exactly
to the point: too many moderns try to be unshackled and
succeed only in being unbuttoned.

The principle of obedience to the Highest is written, top and bottom, on the Christian scheme of things. Mind you, to the *Highest!* Submission to the low and the unworthy signifies weakness, not strength. Submission to God signifies strength, not weakness.

It is true that the committed Christian, in whom the mind of Christ is expressing itself, must frequently have a roll-call of his loyalties and strategies. Our obediences have to be "rated": some have a higher priority than others. Christians in the family for example, owe certain loyalties to one another. Yet a Christian son will not lie or rob, even though commanded to do so by an unprincipled father. Christians have citizenship obligations. Yet Christians will not give a blind loyalty to the tyranny of a government that requires him to violate his conscience. Christians have only one absolute loyalty: that which they give to God and His Kingdom. The rest of their loyalties are all relative. In certain circumstances they are expendable.

In the 1930's the Christians of Germany faced an ominous and painful decision. Hitler's take-over reached the point where it was to include the religious faith of the German people. The church must be "Naziized." A Hitlerian version of the Bible must be accepted. The State was to be supreme. Many pastors went along with this usurpation of absolute power by the little man of Munich. But not all. There were the non-co-operating pastors who in 1934 drew up the "Barmen Declaration." It said in effect: "There are limits to what we 'render unto Caesar,' but there are no limits to what we 'render unto God.' In this case there is collision between the two, and God must come first."

Now listen to a commentator who writes a quarter of a century later: "While one country after another in Europe was compromising with Hitler, while the German universities were allowing him to undermine their sense of truth, while the teaching profession failed to withstand his corroding influence, the Confessing Church suffered but survived."

The line has sometimes seemed thin, but across twenty

centuries of church history it has never been broken, of those who say, "We must obey God rather than men."

E. Think, finally, of Christmindedness as the mind of *sacrifice*. If we ask how far our Lord's obedience carried Him. and at what cost, St. Paul's reply is: "obedient unto death, even the death of the cross."

Bishop Moule's comment is worth noting: "The Greek makes it plain that our Lord did not *obey death* but *obeyed the Father* so utterly as even to die."

How, we may ask, does Christ's sacrifice stand related to the sacrifice that we are to make as Christians, if we in fact are possessed by His "mind"? With the New Testament as our sure guide, we are bound to say that His sacrifice was unique in *achievement* but not in *principle*.

What Christ accomplished by the sacrifice of Himself in death is variously set forth in the New Testament. In writing to the Romans Paul puts it this way: "But God commendeth his love toward us, in that while we were yet sinners Christ died for us. Much more then, being now justified by his blood, we shall be saved from wrath through him (5:8, 9). No one else could do *that!*

In writing to the Galatians the Apostle declares: "Christ hath redeemed us from the curse of the law [the condemnation of God's violated will], being made a curse for us: for it is written, Cursed is every one that hangeth on a tree" (3:13). No one else could do *that!*

The writer to the Hebrews states it thus: "but now once in the end of the world [age] hath he appeared to put away sin by the sacrifice of himself" (9:26). No one else could do *that!*

The achievement of Christ crucified and risen stands alone, utterly unapproachable. Sinlessness has come to grips with sin, and broken its power in our behalf.

> "There was no other good enough
> To pay the price of sin;
> He only could unlock the gate
> Of heaven and let us in."

Now we look at the *principle* that lies at the heart of all this. Paul's whole point is that Christ lived and died on the principle of self-offering rather than self-asserting, self-renouncing in place of self-enriching; and this is to be the governing principle of our lives. It goes right back to verse 4: "Let each of you look not only to his own interest, but also to the interests of others."

Even God binds this principle to His heart. The result, eventually, was a cross — and God stretched upon it.

How then does this involve us — who have the name of Christ upon our lips? It means that over our petty, and often squabbly, self-seeking, God has written His No; and over our self-giving, in the spirit of what Paul elsewhere calls a "living sacrifice," God has written His Yes.

If this means loss, we are not to complain. It meant that for Him. If this means wagging tongues and the twisting of our manners and motives into something other than they really are, we are not to be panicked. It was so with Him. If this means that the chapter of sacrificial love has no happy ending (by any test that Mr. Worldly Wiseman would put upon it), we shall not be dismayed. His story ended (or so His enemies thought) in a Roman crucifixion.

And His "mind" is to be ours.

More, it *is* ours if we are surrendered to it, and are allowing the Holy Spirit to weave its splendid strands into the fabric of our living.

Self-emptied, serving, sympathizing, submitting, sacrificing — a disposition altogether beyond our struggling reach, but not beyond His grace to impart!

Philippians 3

PROFIT AND LOSS: CHRISTIAN STYLE

3:7. "But what things were gain to me, those I counted loss for Christ."

I. HISTORICAL SETTING. Evils of doctrine and of conduct, as we have noted, were not rampant in the Philippian congregation, as they were in the case of the Galatians and the Corinthians. Nevertheless, the threat of trouble was there, and indications of the apostle's concern are not lacking as he writes. In this chapter he directs attention to two perils, the first of which we may call *legalism,* the second, *libertinism.* By the first the gospel was made dangerously narrow, by the second it was made dangerously broad.

Advocates of the first point of view were teachers which New Testament scholars frequently describe as "Judaizers." They insisted on making a hybrid out of the gospel: Christ *and* the law. They wanted a mixture of the cross and circumcision. Mainly these, it is felt, are in Paul's mind as he writes the strong words of verses 2 and 3.

The other danger arises in a different quarter. Those described in the parenthetical sentence of verses 18 and 19 are professing Christians who, presumably under Gnostic influence (or something similar that historically preceded it) have turned the liberty of the Christian man into an immoral license. Here is Christian conduct cut loose from the rigors of obedience to the mind of Christ. Hence Paul's vigorously cautionary word.

There are expositors who hold that a third heresy — perfectionism — is in Paul's view in verses 12-14. While it is clear that Paul wishes to disengage himself from any perfectionist extravagance, there is, as most interpreters appear to recognize, no firm reason for believing that a party or a movement of this character, separable from the legalists and libertarians, was to be found in the congregation.

II. EXPOSITORY MEANING

3:1. After the first sentence of the verse, was the apostle interrupted in his writing and set on a new course in his thinking? By some interpreters this is held to be the case. The theory requires belief that he was troubled by the arrival of news from Philippi later than that which Epaphroditus had brought. Or was this sudden eruption of warning against the "circumcision party" an instance, highly allowable in an informal letter like this, of fresh thoughts forming within his mind in the midst of his writing and now expressed under the sovereign guidance of the Holy Spirit? While no resolution of the two views is likely to occur, it is fair to say that the first opinion is completely without warrant so far as any evidence in the text is concerned. As for the phrase "To write the same things to you," it seems clearly to point to some previous message (or messages) that Paul had sent to the Philippians.

3:2. Three strong epithets: "dogs," "evil workers," "the concision." In Western society we have gone so far in domesticating and sophisticating dogs that those who are fond of these delightful pets find it hard to realize with what contempt they have been treated, by Jews and Gentiles alike, in the Eastern world. There are ancient literary sources that may be used to prove that paying for a dog and hiring a harlot were put in the same category. The word, therefore, when used figuratively as Paul does here, is one of profound contempt. "Concision," which appears nowhere else in Scripture, might be rendered, literally, *mutilation*. The position is: they who insist on circumcision as something essential to salvation are no better than mutilators of the body.

Question: do the three epithets refer to the Judaizers, or do they describe different classes against which the believers must be on guard? If the latter, what are these groups? Some say (1) Gentiles ("dogs"), (2) self-appointed, self-seeking

Christian teachers ("evil workers"), and (3) unbelieving Jews ("the concision"). Most expositors regard this as a needless refinement of interpretation. The more natural construction, they feel, is the one in which Paul simply trebles the condemning account of these troublemakers of the circumcision group.

3:3. In the New Covenant of grace and faith circumcision is of the heart. Its three marks are (1) a vivified worship, (2) a glorified Christ, and (3) a crucified self. The word "spirit" is better understood as a reference to the Holy Spirit, and should therefore be capitalized. When *He* inspires worship, it is authentic. Christ is honored because, far from boasting of men or forms or sects or parties, His enlightened disciples make Him their boast and joy. But if Christ is to have in fact this central place of honor, "the flesh" must be repudiated as a basis for boasting or a foundation for confidence. H. C. G. Moule, in *Philippian Studies,* has a useful comment on the Apostle's use of "flesh:" "The *sarx* (flesh) in Paul is very fairly represented by the word 'self' as used popularly in religious language . . . in such contexts as this, where it stands more or less distinguished from the *pneuma* (spirit), it is not a synonym for 'the body.' Sins of the 'flesh' may be sins purely of the mind, as e.g., 'emulation' (Gal. 5:20)."

3:5. Understand the phrase "an Hebrew of the Hebrews" to mean " a Hebrew sprung from Hebrews." "Though a Hellenist, Paul was trained in the use of the Hebrew tongue by Hebrew-speaking parents" (Vincent).

"A Pharisee." Not all Pharisees were hypocrites. The tradition of the party was that of the most precise and puritanical devotion to the Law.

3:6. Paul uses "blameless" in a relative sense: "blameless," that is, by Pharisaic standards.

3:8. The phrase "that I may win Christ" may easily suffer from too meager an understanding of it. It is better to read "gain" for "win." Paul is drawing up a balance sheet between losses and gains. Acquiring Christ is a "gain" so tremendous, so utterly to be treasured, that Paul is incomparably ahead after letting go the junky values to which he once clung in the futile attempt to make himself acceptable to God. But to "gain" Christ means much more than *finding* Him, or being found by Him, as was true with Paul in the day of his conversion. The "gain" includes the unceasing *increment* of value that one discovers in Him all the way along. Somewhere, years ago, I came on the suggestion that we might well translate this phrase "that I may *amass* Christ." Life with Him is cumulative in value. It mounts in richness. Since there is in Him an infinite dimension and no human experience of Him ever exhausts Him, it is right to say that He is to us a greater and greater Christ as we live in His love and are nourished by His mind.

3:9. By "mine own righteousness" is meant *a righteousness which, by Pharisaic standards, might be called my own.*

3:10. Connect this verse with verse 8. Here it is the spelling out of the meaning that is implicit in the related references to *knowing Christ* and *gaining Christ.* The present participial form is used in the phrase "being made conformable unto His death." The believer's identification with Christ in crucifixion and resurrection may be, indeed should be, *total* from the point of view of *commitment.* Hence the truth of "the crisis of the deeper life." But the identification is never more than *partial* from the point of view of *fulfillment.* Hence the truth in the process of deeper death. Dead to sin? In principle, yes. And now this faith-position of death carries me progressively into all those innumerable and immeasurable crucifixions by which my faulty judgment and ailing memory and faltering courage and pre-occupied thoughts and fatigued or diseased body must be brought into line with the holy madness and the lofty elevation of the cross.

3:11. The alteration (in most later translations) from "of the dead" to "from the dead" is justified. The Greek preposition implies the distinction between the resurrection of the just and the resurrection of the unjust. It may or may not imply *all* of the differences between the two that are worked out in some schemes of eschatology. The "if" clause poses a problem only for those whose schematic theology is more rigid than Holy Scripture itself. It thus may be taken to have a meaning that avoids two unbiblical extremes: (1) a constant struggle with doubt about our eventually being among the saved, and (2) a presumptuous abdication of believer's responsibility in favor of unconditional divine election and predestination. As timely as it is sound is an appeal by Professor John Murray of Westminster Theological Seminary: "Let us appreciate the doctrine of the perseverance of the saints and recognize that we may entertain the faith of our security in Christ only as we persevere in faith and holiness to the end."

3:12. Precise interpretation of the first clause turns on two pivots: (1) Is this a flashback to verse 10, where the stress is on knowledge of Christ? or (2) is it a reference to verse 11, where the picture is that of reaching the future goal of participation in the resurrection and its consummating blessedness? If the former, then it would appear to be a perfection of spiritual knowledge or experience that Paul disavows; if the latter, then clearly the disclaimer relates to resurrection felicity and "finishedness." The use of "attain" in verses 11 and 12 superficially favors the second view. The case for it, however, is weakened by the fact that two *different* words are used in the Greek. Competent New Testament scholars can be quoted in support of each view. In the end, what really matters is that the Apostle simply will not have it that any testimony of his either claims or implies that his Christian character is complete or his Christian course finished. The concluding "if" clause is more lucidly rendered in all of our later versions: e.g., Phillips, "grasping ever more firmly that purpose for which Christ grasped me," or Vincent, "I am pressing on toward the attainment and fulfillment of that which Christ contemplated in my conversion."

3:14. Are the "prize" and the "high calling" the same, or are they distinct? If they are the same, we shall understand Paul to be saying, in effect, "I press toward the mark for that prize which takes the form of my heavenly calling." If the second interpretation is ours, as it is mine, then the picture called up by Paul's athletic figure of speech is that of the runner reaching the "goal," the winning line, and then, as reward for his victory, receiving the traditional garland or wreath from the king. The reward is a "crown," that is, a share in the glory of the exalted Christ.

3:15. Unless the phrase "as many as be perfect" is a contradiction of verse 12, we must assign a double meaning to the word translated "perfect." *There* it means the completed Christian man, including the resurrection body; here it means the Christian man who, by the grace of God, has in fact entered that spiritual adulthood in which with single-mindedness he moves from one degree of progress and perfection to another. We must avoid the attempt to soften the Pauline demand for evangelical (that is, the by-grace-through-faith) perfection by settling for some vague maturation process. Paul sees those who *are* "mature." He sees those who *are* "spiritual" (cf. I Cor. 2:15, 3:1).

3:18. These, it would appear, are not the legalists of verse 2. These are the libertarians. The former debase grace by mixing works with it; the latter pervert grace by divorcing it from behavior.

3:20. "Conversation" leads us astray. Better rendered, as in several later versions, "citizenship." The meaning: as the *seat* of citizenship for colonial Philippi is Rome, so the seat and center of the life of Christians in Philippi is "heaven." The "we look" suggests eagerness and intensity.

3:21. Neither the "vile body" of the Authorized Version nor the "wretched bodies" of Phillips is a happy translation. Much to be preferred is "our lowly body" (RSV) or "the body of our humiliation" (Moule and others). It is a body not in itself evil but bearing the marks of frailty and mortality as compared with the "body of glory" which it will become by refashioning at the resurrection.

III. DOCTRINAL VALUE. Upon three areas of theological concern this chapter throws light: (1) the Christian understanding of grace (which rules out the legalism of circumcision), (2) the doctrine of evangelical perfection according to which God does in fact give to His people a verifiable maturity which must then be held *in tension* with their

manifest imperfection, the latter requiring all the vigilance
and discipline of unceasing growth in order to cope with it,
and (3) the "blessed hope" of Christ's coming again.

IV. PRACTICAL AIM. Two purposes, both of them ad-
monitory, may be said to lie behind what our author has to
say in Chapter 3: (1) a warning against the folly and futility
of salvation by works and (2) a warning against the folly and
futility of professing a salvation which, making light of
works, falls into lawlessness and anarchy. Here are the oppo-
site perils of legalism and libertinism. Against both Paul
would fortify the church by strengthening the confidence of
the believers in the Christ who, having given the church His
boundless life in love, governs it in His binding lordship.

V. HOMILETICAL FORM

Theme: "Profit and Loss: Christian Style."

Introduction: What is *your scale* of values?

Each of us has one. We may be reflective about it or not.
We may or may not try to put it in words. In any case it is
there — shaping, coloring, controlling our lives.

For five years a professor in a Texas university has put a
simple questionnaire before his Freshman students. One of
its three questions is: "Is there anything you would be willing to die for? If so, what is it?" With a regularity that would
have been monotonous if it had not been so appalling, the
reply was "No." At the beginning of the sixth year of this
experiment one Freshman wrote: "I would be willing to die
for my family."

When asked in Question Two about the things they would
like to change in their present situation, a high percentage
of the answers ran in the direction of "more money to spend"
or "two cars instead of one."

Values! This man Paul has a thing or two to say about
values. Even in his pre-Christian days he put a higher store
by the higher values than do a shocking number of America's
college students. Still, the whole point of what Paul is saying
in our text is that when he met Jesus Christ his scheme of

values underwent a tremendous change. His language is that
of the market-place or the corporation's directors' meeting:
profit and loss. "What things were gain to me, those I
counted loss for Christ." And in the next breath he makes it
even stronger: "I have suffered the loss of all things, and do
count them but dung, that I may win [that is, gain] Christ."

Paul is fond of this manner of speaking:

"Renouncing all, I recover all."

"Giving up everything *for* Christ, I find everything *in*
Christ."

"Admitting my rags, I am invested with His riches."

Now what in fact did Paul "gain" through this exchange in
which an old life of his was given up and a new life in
Christ was received?

A. He acquired an *identity* that he regarded as highly
distinctive.

Ask him for his old identity, and he can give you a variety
of answers: a properly "circumcised" Israelite! a member of
"the tribe of Benjamin!" no proselyte but a full-blooded
"Hebrew!" a law-keeping "Pharisee!"

Address him by any of these titles, and he could nod his
acknowledgment.

But a great change had come to him. Tennyson has those
plaintive lines:

> "And ah for a man to arise in me,
> That the man I am may cease to be!"

The man that Paul *was* had "ceased to be." And the new
man that had arisen in place of the old found that all he
wanted was to be known as Christ's man: Christ's "servant,"
Christ's "apostle," Christ's "ambassador."

Christ's man, Paul contends, participates in a distinctive
ritual. Of himself and his fellow believers he testifies: "we
are the circumcision, which worship God in the spirit," or, as
the American Standard Version has it in its alternative reading, "we are the true circumcision, who worship by the spirit
of God" (v. 3). I am done forever, says Paul, with the smug
feeling that any external rite in itself — be it circumcision or

baptism — makes me acceptable to God as I offer myself to Him in worship. It is by the Spirit of God that I am perpetually reminded of my unworthiness, perpetually assured of my cleansing, and perpetually prepared to offer acceptable praise and prayer to the God who looks not on "the outward appearance" but "upon the heart."

More than this, Christ's man engages in a distinctive sort of *rejoicing*. Paul and his comrades "rejoice in Christ Jesus" (v. 3).

Are you awed by the nave and apse and altar of a cathedral? Some are; some are not. Are you moved by the solemn pageantry of an eleborately formal Communion Service? Some are; some are repelled.

Whatever the case the ultimate thrill for the sensitive Christian is not in symbol but in the reality symbolized, Isaac Watts wrote of it:

> "Not all the blood of beasts,
>   On Jewish altars slain,
> Could give the guilty conscience peace,
>   Or wash away our stain.
> But Christ, the heavenly Lamb,
>   Takes all our sins away;
> A sacrifice of nobler name,
>   And richer blood than they.
> Believing, we rejoice,
>   To see the curse removed;
> We bless the Lamb with cheerful voice,
>   And sing His bleeding love."

And another thing, says Paul: Christ's man practices a distinctive *renunciation*. They who are in Christ "have no confidence in the flesh" (v 3). The apostle's frequent references to "the flesh" have given rise to some foolish statements, even among those who have been students of his life. I cannot find any evidence that his peculiar weakness lay in the area of sex, as some have suggested. This kind of interpretation misses the special, *ethical* meaning that the expression bears in most — though not all — of the passages in which it occurs. It stands for human nature viewed either in its defiance of God's will and order for human life or in its failure to submit completely, in principle at least, to that order. It is plain old *ego* in whatever subtle form it may disguise its intention to have its way.

That, says Paul, has been renounced, is being renounced, and must continue to be renounced. Confidence put in self is always misplaced; confidence put in Christ need never be replaced.

Here, then, is the distinctive identity that Paul has gained by consenting to the loss of those tinsel prizes on which self would dote.

B. Paul has gained an *intimacy* that is remunerative. Saul of Tarsus was a man struggling feverishly to keep a law and conform to a code. Paul of Damascus — the Christian Paul — was a man discovering the sheer joy and strength of fellowship with a Person.

Listen to him as he declares, not self-pityingly but exultantly, "Indeed I count everything as loss because of the surpassing worth of knowing Christ Jesus my Lord" (v. 8, RSV). "This personal union with Christ," says New Testament scholar A. E. Garvie, "is the constant dominating factor in the religious experience and moral character of Paul." And Barclay reminds us that Paul's Greek word for "know" means "not simply intellectual knowledge.... It is the personal experience of another person."

Note Paul's three reasons for feeling that such personal experience of Christ is "gain":

First, because *it brings us acceptance with God.* The testimony of verse 9 lights up this point: "that I may gain Christ, and be found in Him, not having a righteousness of my own, based on law, but that which is through faith in Christ, the righteousness from God which depends on faith" (RSV). Righteousness as God's gift, not man's achievement, is at the center of the gospel. The assured basis for it is what Christ has done on our behalf on the Cross, but the appropriated blessing of it lies in what Christ means to us now through trusting His promise and through the operation of His Spirit.

> "Then take with rejoicing from Jesus at once
> The life everlasting He gives;
> And know with assurance, thou never canst die
> Since Jesus, thy Righteousness, lives."

Secondly, intimacy with Christ does more than bring us acceptance with God: *it bends us to the pattern of the Cross.* Listen now as Paul describes the sustained, creative longing of his redeemed soul: "that I may know Him and the power of His resurrection, and may share His sufferings, becoming like Him in His death" (v. 10, RSV).

It was a flaming Maclaren of Manchester, preaching to a previous generation, who warned and pled: "The world's war-cries today are two — 'Get!' 'Enjoy!' Christ's command is 'Renounce!' and in renouncing we shall realize both of these other aims, which they who pursue them only never attain."

Life in its Christian fashion is always *cruciform*. It is easy to say the word. Only the indwelling Christ Himself can, through us, fill out the pattern.

Thirdly, this intimacy with Christ *binds us by the law of faith.* The double reference to faith in verse 9 is characteristic of Paul. It is by faith that the Apostle is "found in Him" (Christ) and there, in such a life-union, God's righteousness becomes his, not because he struggles to keep the law but because he trusts the law-fulfilling Savior.

Eighteen centuries after Paul, another groping spirit made a similar discovery. His name was John Wesley. Unlike Paul, he had a Christian background. Like him, however, he found that a religion of rite and rote, of form without life and creed without flame, even though it bear the name "Christian," yields no peace.

Then came Aldersgate — a May night in 1738 when Wesley was listening to a man read from Luther's Preface to Paul's Letter to the Romans! Let Wesley's own words tell it: "While he was describing the change which God works in the heart through faith in Christ, I felt my heart strangely warmed. I felt that I did trust in Christ, Christ alone, for salvation: and an assurance was given me that He had taken away my sins, even mine, and saved me from the laws of sin and death."

Both Paul and Wesley learned that whereas the law of works brings frustration, the law of faith brings freedom.

Looking at Paul's balance sheet, we have seen that, as he views it, his profits have far outweighed his losses. He has gained an identity that is distinctive and an intimacy that is remunerative.

Come now for a final look at his ledger.

C. Paul has gained *an expectancy* that is exhilarative. This forward look shows itself in verse 11 and is described with a kind of explicit radiance in verse 20. In the former he unveils his heart's hope "to attain the resurrection from the dead." In the latter he links this happy event with the return of Christ: "But our commonwealth is in heaven, and from it we await a Saviour, the Lord Jesus Christ, who will change our lowly body to be like His glorious body, by the power which enables Him even to subject all things to Himself" (RSV).

Like jewels on a fine, firm thread, here are three related thoughts.

The sure return! "From it [heaven] we await a Saviour." He went away. He promised to come again. It is our unshakable hope that He will.

The splendid redemption! He "will change our lowly body to be like His glorious body." For all its wonder of structure and functioning, it is a "lowly body." It is fettered by frailties, locked within limitations, pursued by pain, doomed to die. Lowly indeed!

But the resurrection will reverse all of that: frailties ended, limitations lifted, pain banished, death itself destroyed!

John Donne's lines are as Biblical as they are brilliant, as Pauline as they are polished:

> "Death be not proud, though some have called thee
> Mighty and dreadful, for, thou art not so:
> For those whom thou thinkest thou dost overthrow
> Die not, poor Death; not yet canst thou kill me . . .
> Thou art slave to fate, chance, kings, and desperate men,

And dost with poison, war, and sickness dwell;
And poppy or charms can make us sleep as well
And better than thy stroke. Why swell'st then?
    One short sleep past, we wake eternally,
    And Death shall be no more: Death, thou shalt die!"

And then — lest all this be held impossible — *the sufficient resource!* That resource, Paul assures us, is nothing less than "the power which enables him even to subject all things to himself." He gave us the earnest of His ultimate victory when He Himself rose from the dead. For a believer like Paul that triumph of an enemy-vanquishing yesterday is proof enough of a larger triumph yet to be when, with sunrise gladness, this mortal puts on immortality and this corruptible puts on incorruption.

Ah, Paul, you must be right!

Such "gains" as these far eclipse your losses.

A new identity! I am Christ's.

A new intimacy! He opens His heart to me — as He does to all who will believe it — and I live in His love.

A new expectancy! "The best is yet to be."

Philippians 4

HOW TO SAY "I CAN"

4:13. "I can do all things through Christ which strength-eneth me."

I. HISTORICAL SETTING. Paul will now deal with a threatening rift in the fellowship of the Philippian congregation. He will then take exquisitely grateful notice of the gift which his friends at Philippi had sent to him, his gratitude enhanced by the fact that this was not the first time they had given him financial assistance. Finally, he will let it be known that Christ has His witness right in the palace of the Caesar in Rome.

II. EXPOSITORY MEANING

4:2. "Beseech" is repeated in connection with each name. Full translation would be: "Euodias I exhort and Syntyche I exhort." A separate message is conveyed to each of them, imploring them to "make up their differences," if we may borrow J. B. Phillips' language, and thus to be "of the same mind."

4:3. "Yokefellow" means simply comrade or, since the Greek word permits it, it may be a proper name for some one whose identity can be only a subject for speculation. Among the identifications suggested: Paul's wife, Timothy, Silas, Luke, or the chief bishop at Philippi.

4:5. "Moderation" is better rendered "forbearance." Paul's word combines the ideas of *patience* and *sweetness*: hence Wuest's translation of "sweet reasonableness," though this sounds a bit too saccharine to be Pauline.

"The Lord is at hand" splits the commentators, for the most part, into two camps: (1) those who hold it to be an equivalent of the Christian watchword in Aramaic, *Mara-natha,* "the Lord cometh," and (2) those who regard it as Paul's reference to the immediate and intimate nearness of the Lord, after the fashion of Psalm 119:151 or Psalm 34:18. Remarkably enough, two ardent believers in the doctrine of Christ's Second Advent and its imminency (F. B. Meyer and Harry Ironside) held the second interpretation. On either view the grammatical question remains: Does Paul intend that we take these words in their *backward* or their *forward* direction? If the former, they are an incentive to patience and magnanimity; if the latter, to restfulness and poise.

4:6. "Careful." Caffin says it means "anxious, distracting care," though Vincent holds that it does not always bear this meaning in the New Testament.

"Prayer and supplication:" only Paul among New Testament writers joins the two, the distinction being that "prayer" is the general term and "supplication" the specific petition which in each case we may be guided to make.

4:7. "Passeth all understanding." If Lightfoot and Vincent are right, Paul is not precisely saying that God's peace in the soul is unfathomable, or incomprehensible; he is saying, rather, that it affords a quietness that "overtops" (literally), or surpasses, the serenity we try to achieve through our "cleverness" or "ingenuity." Either view may be taken; the second seems to suit the context better.

4:8. "Honest" is better rendered "venerable," or, since that has overtones of age, "worthy of reverence."

"Pure." The Greek is strong; purity through and through, "motives as well as acts," as Vincent observes.

"Good report" is better rendered, as in Weymouth, "worthy of praise."

"Any virtue," that is, any moral excellence of any kind (as grounded in the goodness of God).

"Think" in the sense of "fix your minds."

4:10. "Flourish" is to be taken in the sense of "revive" or "blossom."

"Ye were also careful." Imperfect tense, meaning "you were all along thinking of me."

4:11. "Learned." The Greek tense is aorist, suggesting not a vague process of learning but a *time* when the secret was imparted to him, which could mean the time when he became a Christian or in some subsequent crisis.

"Content." Not purely placidity, but *independence of circumstances;* it is the Stoic ideal of self-sufficiency Christianized, that is, grounded not in self but in Christ.

4:12. "Instructed." "Learned the secret" (RSV).

4:14. "Nevertheless." As a connective its logic is, "Do not think that, because I am independent of external circumstances, I lightly regard the help you send."

"Well" is a weak rendering; better translated "nobly."

"Communicate" is rarely used today in the older sense of "share," which is the rendering preferred by most modern translators.

4:15. "The beginning of the gospel," that is, its first proclamation in Macedonia.

4:17. Exquisite courtesy here, in which, having already disclaimed any crippling sense of want, Paul now disclaims desire for a gift which could be considered valuable for its own sake; he is interested chiefly in the enriching reward that will accrue to the givers.

4:22. "They that are of Caesar's household." Not necessarily, or even probably, members of the royal family, but *slaves* and *civil servants.* Lightfoot thinks there were converts who had already confessed the Christian faith when Paul came to Rome.

III. DOCTRINAL VALUE. The chapter, while belonging to the practical part of the epistle, contains, by implication, an exhilarating study in the doctrine of Providence. "What is called providence," wrote Calvin, "describes God, not as idly beholding from heaven the transactions which happen in the world, but as holding the helm of the universe, and regulating all events" (Institutes of the Christian Religion, Book I, ch. 16). Writing on *Divine Providence,* John Wesley observed that God "is concerned every moment for what befalls every creature upon earth; and more especially for everything

that befalls any of the children of men" (Vol. 6, p. 317) . It
is in this context of understanding that Paul is able to testify
as he does in this chapter.

IV. PRACTICAL AIM. First to forestall a serious breach in
the fellowship and unity of the Christian group in Philippi;
secondly, to encourage faith in the utter reliability and the
infinite resourcefulness of God as He has revealed Himself in
Jesus Christ; and, thirdly, to express deepest gratitude to the
Philippians for the gift they sent him.

V. HOMILETICAL FORM
   Theme: "How to Say 'I Can.' "

   Introduction: It is never hard to find people who know
how to say, "I can't." They are the completely frustrated or
more than half-defeated souls who make up a sad proportion
of the populace in any man's town — including its church
members.
   Listen to their talk:
   "I can't control my temper." "I can't keep my thoughts
clean." "I can't concentrate on my work." "I can't stay
sober." "I can't pray in public." "I can't make a success of
my job." "I can't tithe my income for the Kingdom of God."
"I can't live victoriously." "I can't keep worry out of my
mind." "I can't stand my mother-in-law."
   The list is almost endless. You have heard it all many
times. And will you say that you have not at some time
joined the wretched chorus yourself?
   "I can't. . . I can't. . . I can't!"
   With some of us, it is a habit that hog-ties us. It is a mood
that masters us. It is a mentality that produces fatality. Every
hope of radiant, adequate living is choked off.
   Contrast all this with the spirit and outlook of our text.
   Here is a man who says, "I can!" Just how he says it, and
with what meaning, are matters that will concern us as we go
along. For the moment the big bracing thing that confronts
us is the *fact* that he says it.
   And now, as the "newscasters" sometimes say, the details!

A. It is *important* that we learn to say what Paul said —
"I can."

As a matter of fact — and this will come as a shock to some
of you — it is more important to say "I can" than to say "I
will." This is especially true when we face responsibilities or
challenges in which the emotions are strongly involved. It is
true also when, over an extended period of time, the sub-
conscious mind has been fed a long stream of negative thinking and has become a receptacle for the after-effects of defeats
and failures.

My meaning will be clearer, I hope, if I appeal to an incident described by a doctor who had a great deal of experience with war casualties in World War I. The doctor treated
a lad of twenty who was invalided home from battle in Italy,
where he was paralyzed in both legs. The physical disable-
ment cleared up. Nevertheless, when the patient attempted
to walk, he failed. Even his most determined efforts to stand
alone ended in failure and humiliation. Being convinced that
there was no actual disease of the nervous system, the doctor,
who was a neurologist, decided to treat the young soldier
under hypnosis. In hypnosis, of course, the direct appeal of
the hypnotist is to the unconscious mind. In this case the
unconscious mind was assured that the normal use of the
legs *was* possible. The outcome? In a few weeks the young
man was playing football!

The case is unusual, let us admit, but the point it illus-
trates applies in varying degrees to most of us. The young
man's victory did not lie so much in "I will" as it lay in "I
can." At the deepest level it was *faith-power* rather than
will-power. The importance of that principle can hardly be
exaggerated. "Everything," says Jesus, "everything is 'can' to
him that believeth."

B. It is *imperative* that we say "I can" in the right way.

The right way, let me quickly add, is the Christian —
Paul's way.

Suppose Paul had stopped when he said "I can do all
things." If the period had come at that point, these five

little words would have been monosyllables of madness. The man who says "I can do all things" commits two sins in one breath: the sin of falsehood and the sin of conceit.

And yet to hear some people talk today about "the power of positive thinking" gives you the impression that they are going to conquer themselves and the world by means of this magic formula which is calculated to wake up all the hidden powers locked up in themselves.

I do not deny for a moment that most of us have powers of mind and body far beyond anything we are actually utilizing. The Creator has endowed us with them and they are part of our nature. Most of us are content to run our intellectual and physical engine on about half of the cylinders.

But here is the hitch: if you are dependent only on powers that you wake up within yourself, *you* are at the center, not Christ. With Paul it was not so. The all-conquering strength of which he speaks was not centered in him; it was centered in the Lord Jesus Christ within him. The difference between these two ways of experiencing mastery is tremendous. In one case you are the "big cheese" and you end up as the big chaff; in the other case He is the big Strengthener and you end up as the big receiver. *"In Him who strengthens me, I am able for anything,"* is the way Moffatt translates our text. In myself — some things; in Him — everything! My mastery is to be mastered by Him. My adequacy is to be adequately surrendered to Him. This, the Christian contends, is the right way to say "I can."

C. It is *impressive* to examine the range of our possibilities when we say "I can" in the Christian way.

For one thing, says Paul, I can *love*. I can love where it is not natural to love — where unlove, dislike, and even hatred, are often found. Ponder these words of verse 1: *"My brethren dearly beloved and longed for, my joy and crown ... my dearly beloved."* Moffatt has it, *"those for whom I cherish love and longing."*

Who were these people for whom the apostle cherished so tender a regard? They were people who did not belong to his race or nation. He was a Jew and they were Gentiles. Until they were changed by the power of the gospel that Paul preached to them, they had been pagans. So intense and self-sacrificing was Paul's love for them that he had suffered to within an inch of his life to bring Christ to them. It was in Philippi, you remember, that Paul and Silas had been so cruelly beaten and brutally jailed. Yet the love of Christ in them conquered all: a Christian church was established in that corrupt city.

The victory of love in Paul can become the victory of love in you. With the love of unfailing and creative good-will, you can love that unlovely person. You can love that hard-to-love individual.

In India a young man from a wealthy Hindu family became a Christian. The rest of the family, bitterly opposed to Christianity, said, "We will take away your share in the inheritance." Completely unembittered, he let them do it. But soon they were quarreling among themselves over his share. Finally, in order to break the deadlock, they asked him to step in as mediator, since he was the only one that all of them could trust. There he sat, arbitrating the distribution of property, stolen from him! Most of us would have said, "I can't, and I won't." Not he. With a heart saturated with Calvary-love he said, "I can" — and he did. He later became the Prime Minister of one of the great states of India.

There's something else I may do when I have learned the Christian way of saying "I can." I can *heal*. I can be used by the Spirit of God to bring harmony where there is discord, reconciliation where there is strife.

Consider the situation in the Philippian Church. According to verse 2, there was a misunderstanding between two lady members of that congregation. Perhaps they had been acting a bit unladylike, for Paul says, as Phillips renders it, *"Euodias and Syntyche I beg you by name to make up your differences as Christians should!"*

Then, in the following verse, the Apostle addresses some unknown leader in the church (perhaps Luke, as Ramsay suggests), urging him to "help those women." That is, help them to get together "in the Lord." Help them to end this bickering, this mischievous tiff that keeps them apart and tends to divide the whole congregation.

There is a healing ministry that lies open to all of us when we have taken to ourselves the secret of saying, "I can." If there is a falling out in the family, or among the neighbors, or in the church, what do you do? Do you go around to Mrs. Longears and say, "Have you heard about Mrs. Euodias and Mrs. Syntyche? They're on the outs with each other. Isn't it just terrible?" And you and Mrs. Longears smack your lips over that word "terrible." Instead of that kind of useless talk, you can do something constructive. You can pray that this friction will end. You can do something more. You can ask God if He wants to guide you directly to these persons and there, in humble love, to appeal to them to resolve their differences in the spirit of Christ. You can talk *about* them — anybody can do that. But also, you can talk *to* them — Christ in you will enable you to do that.

Remember that simple, lovely prayer by Francis of Assisi:
"Lord, make me an instrument of Thy peace:
    Where there is hatred, let me sow love.
    Where there is injury, let me sow pardon.
    Where there is doubt, let me sow faith.
    Where there is despair, let me sow hope.
    Where there is darkness, let me sow light.
    Where there is sadness, let me sow joy."

Yes, I *can* be a healer!

There is still another thing I can do. I can be *glad*. Verse 4 says it: "Rejoice in the Lord alway; and again I say, Rejoice." Will you try to remember that the man who said that was writing down his thoughts in prison?

You see the gladness of the Christian is gladness *in spite of!* In spite of fetters, and foulness, and friendlessness!

But the Christian's gladness is also gladness *because of!* Because of "the Lord!" Not because of prosperity, or popularity, or pleasure, but because of the Lord who had nothing of this and yet could say, "These things have I spoken unto you that my joy might be in you and that your joy might be full" (John 15:11).

True the Christian's joy is not necessarily a boisterous hilarity or a bubbling ecstasy. Paul's friend, Seneca, hit it about right when he said: "True joy is a serene and sober motion, and they are miserably out who take laughing for rejoicing."

John Keble, in a St. Matthews' Day poem, once put it beautifully;

> "There are in this loud, stunning tide
> Of human care and crime,
> Those with whom the melodies abide
> Of the everlasting chime;
> Who carry music in their heart,
> Through dusty lane and wrangling mart,
> Plying their daily task with busier feet
> Because their secret souls some holy strain repeat."

So, put it down among all the things that I can do through Christ which strengtheneth me: I can be *glad!*

Once more, I can be *patient.* Look at verse 5: "Let your moderation be known unto all men." Williams translates it: *"Let your forbearing spirit be known to everybody."* The dictionary will tell you that forbearance is "patience, self-control."

A finer shading of the Greek word here suggests the ability to yield to others. The yielding, of course, is to be taken in a noble, not an ignoble, sense. Christ's man never yields his principles or his convictions. On the other hand, he often finds it wise to yield his prejudices, or his preferences, or his pleasures, or even his rights.

John Wesley and a notorious agnostic found themselves coming at each other on a narrow foot-bridge. The agnostic, recognizing the famous Mr. Wesley, glowered at him and said, "I never give way to a fool." John Wesley, stepping politely aside, said smilingly, "My friend, I always do!"

When patience was required, in place of wounded pride or flaring anger, the pious Mr. Wesley was able to say, "I can... I can!"

Here we must stop, not because we have exhausted the possibilities of the Christ-empowered life but for sheer lack of space. The ability to love, to heal, to be glad, to be patient — these are but samples of that limitless gift of power that is ours in Jesus Christ.

Paul goes on to say, "I can be *calm*," for "the peace of God, which passeth all understanding keeps my heart" (v. 7).

"I can *think*, and think as a Christian, for the things that are "true," and "honest," and "pure," and "lovely," and "of good report," are mine to feed upon (v. 8).

I can be *satisfied*, for "I have learned in whatsoever state I am, therewith to be content" (v. 11).

In fine, "I can do *all things* through Christ which strengtheneth me."

As a kind of footnote to this testimony by the Apostle there's a short sentence full of meaning that is tucked away back in verse 5: "The Lord is at hand," or as Phillips puts it, *"Never forget the nearness of your Lord."*

But that, I suspect, is exactly where some of us have failed. That is where we have missed — or lost — the secret of saying "I can." We have forgotten the nearness of our Lord.

Perhaps we have never really let Him come near and make Himself our very own Saviour. Perhaps, if we have, there has been a forgetting of His nearness. Or perhaps His nearness could be a much greater thing to us if only we let Him have *all* there is of us.

In any case, let Him have you for what you are — a miserable piece of futility and failure in yourself. And let Him give Himself to you for what He is — a source of strength unfailing, a secret of victory which knows no defeat.

The Epistle to the Colossians

Colossians 1

MAN WITH A MESSAGE

1:25. "I am made a minister ... to fulfill the word of God."

I. HISTORICAL SETTING. Paul addresses a community of Christians who, almost certainly, were never visited by him. Through Epaphras, however, he has learned of their faith and testimony. Epaphras, who may have been the founder of the church, has also reported the peril to the faith that has arisen from a group within the community who have adopted what New Testament scholars have come to describe as "the Colossian heresy." It seems to have combined three distinguishable ingredients: (1) something of Jewish legalism, with a demand for the observance of certain feasts and fasts; (2) something of Greek philosophy, with a high view of the spiritual and a low view of the material, developing (later) into a complex scheme in which God, being holy, is relieved of the responsibility for having created the material order; and (3) something of mystic enlightenment, in which the "initiated" entered upon a knowledge "denied the many and reserved for the few." The nub of the whole problem, as Paul saw it, was that this error threatened the sovereignty and sufficiency of Jesus Christ as God self-revealed and solitary Saviour.

II. EXPOSITORY MEANING

1:5. "For," in the Greek has the force of *on account of.* Hence the question has been raised as to whether the phrase it introduces should be connected with the "the love ... to all the saints" or referred back to the "we give thanks" of verse 3. An objection to the first view is that it seems to make "love," which in the highest Christian sense supplies its own motives, depend for motivation on the "hope" of future reward. The text itself is not decisive.

1.6. "In all the world." Called by Ellicott an "intelligible hyperbole" because, first of all, the penetration of the gospel Paul has in mind would be, most obviously, the Roman world of that day, and, further, because the gospel, considered in its nature and intent, is universal.

1.8. "Your love in the Spirit." Well rendered by Weymouth, "your love, which is inspired by the Holy Spirit."

1:9. "Wisdom and spiritual understanding." On the distinction between the two Barclay has a remark which, though it may not plumb the depths, is admirable for the simplicity of it, "When Paul prays that his friends may have *wisdom* and *understanding,* he is praying that they may understand the great truths of Christianity, and that they may be able to apply these truths to the tasks and decisions which meet them in everyday living."

1:10. "Unto all pleasing" is by Moule rendered "to all meeting of His wishes." "Give him entire satisfaction" is the Moffatt translation.

1:12. "Meet." *Made fit, qualified.*

"The inheritance of the saints in light": God's kingdom is a kingdom of light; in that kingdom each believer has, through Christ, a portion.

1:14. "Through his blood" is omitted from most modern versions because of weak manuscript authority for it, but the Pauline view of atonement is not thereby altered since, on the firmest manuscript grounds, the phrase appears in verse 20.

1:15. "Image." The learned Bishop Nicholson, in his notes on Colossians, suggests that three ideas combine in this word — *derivation, representation, manifestation;* that is, Christ comes from God, represents God, unveils God. "The firstborn of every creature" not justifying the contention of the Jehovah's Witnesses that this makes Christ a created being, but, as A. M. Hunter has pointed out, "The phrase means 'One who was in being before creation'; and, since primogeniture implied superior dignity, the thought is that Christ is prior in dignity, as well as in time, to all created things."

1:17. "Before." That is, prior to, whether in time or rank. "Consist" is better rendered "cohere."

1:18. "The first born from the dead." Already described as chief, or sovereign, of all creation (v. 15), Christ is now portrayed as chief, or head, of the new creation, the community of the redeemed, of which headship His resurrection is a superlative sign, for, as Charles Erdman remarks, "Christ was the first to rise from the dead never to die again."

1:20. "Reconcile." A Greek word which, in root, meant simply to *change,* to be *other,* or *different;* by adding a prefix it came to mean *exchange* or *transform,* and thus it evolved into a term descriptive of what happens when broken or hostile relationships between two parties are *repaired, put right, healed over.*

"All things." Though not fully spelled out by Paul, the fullest meaning should be read into it which does not involve the New Testament in self-contradiction; an example of an unwarranted, because contradictory, view would be that of Origen, who held that "all things" must include the devil and fallen angels. Still, the potency of Paul's affirmation must not be weakened: there is something cosmic about the cross. It has not been the same universe since Christ died and rose again.

1:23. "If." The conditional clause is to be understood in its most natural sense, namely, that if salvation is all of grace, it is also all of faith; and, as Eadie puts it. "The loss of faith is the knell of hope."

1:24. "Fill up that which is behind of the afflictions of Christ." May be taken to mean (1) the sufferings Paul must undergo for the church in sympathy or affinity with the sufferings of Christ or (2) the sufferings that Christ must feel in and through His servant Paul. Obviously, far from Paul's mind here is the expiatory, or atoning, suffering of the Saviour.

1:26. "Mystery." In the New Testament uniformly used in reference to a truth "undiscoverable except by revelation."

III. DOCTRINAL VALUE. Supremely the chapter is distinguished by its profound theological setting forth of the divine-human Person and the uniquely redemptive Work of Jesus Christ. It also introduces us to the doctrine of our "union with Christ" in the saved life, which J. S. Stewart, in *A Man In Christ,* has called "the heart of Paul's religion."

IV. PRACTICAL AIM. By exalting "the sole sufficiency" of Christ, Paul would prepare the Colossian believers to ward off the specious arguments and appeals of the errorists, who insisted that to faith in Christ must be added a curious mixture of Jewish ritual, ascetic austerity, and astrological reliance. The chapter's purpose, which was also the purpose of the entire letter, and indeed Paul's whole ministry, is well stated in verse 28: "warning every man and teaching every man in all wisdom; that we may present every man perfect in Christ Jesus."

V. HOMILETICAL FORM

Theme: "Man with a Message."

Introduction: Some years ago *Fortune* magazine carried a stinging editorial on "The Failure of the Church." "We are asked," wrote the editor, "to turn to the Church for our enlightenment, but when we do so, we find that the voice of the Church is not inspired. The voice of the Church today, we find, is the echo of our own voices."

Today's preaching. Clever? Yes. Analytical? Yes. Problem-conscious? Yes. Socially concerned? Yes.

But it can be all this and be nothing more than an acho of the *New York Times,* or the *Harvard Business Review,* or the *Atlantic Monthly,* or *The Reporter.*

Someone once described Matthew Arnold as "a mournful evangelist who had somehow contrived to mislay his gospel."

Is *that* what has happened to much of contemporary preaching?

Let us face it: it happened to *some* preaching in the first century of the Christian era.

But never to Paul's!

I did not choose this calling, he cries. The calling chose

me. To use his own words, "I am made a minister," and, as such, my business is to "fulfill the word of God." I have no other business — none at least that could ever serve as a substitute for this.

Consider, then, the message of this man Paul.

A. For one thing, it was the message of a *Person*. In verse 27 see how he lifts up the exalted title of "Christ" and then says, "whom we preach."

Not "what," mind you, but "whom." Oh, I know perfectly well that his preaching had a "what" — a logical and theological woof — but the warp was the personal Christ,

> "Fount of life and fire,
> Surpassing all the joys we know,
> And all we can desire."

Christianity is many things — organizations, institutions, rituals, theologies, traditions — but the gospel is Christ. Preaching is never merely talking about Christ. It is Christ Himself being ministered to the people.

It was, of course, as *Saviour* and *Lord* that Paul proclaimed Christ. Colossal, no less, was the figure the apostle saw when he looked at Jesus. Listen to his language in a fine paraphrase such as we have from Phillips: "Now Christ is the visible expression of the invisible God. He existed before creation began, for it was through Him that everything was made, whether spiritual or material, seen or unseen. Through Him, and for Him, also, were created power and dominion, ownership and authority. In fact, every single thing was created through and for Him. He is both the First Principle and the Upholding Principle of the whole scheme of creation" (vv. 15-17).

There were heretics in Colossae — forerunners of the later Gnostics — who had gone off the deep end in their curious doctrine of creation. They were down on matter, holding it to be evil. God, being good, did not create it. It was produced by lower grades of supernatural beings, called *aeons*. Paul brushes this speculative scheme to one side. That there is evil in the universe Paul never denied. He only denied that it is an evil universe. And he insisted that this is a *uni*verse, not a *multi*verse — though the term is ours, not his.

His argument in this chapter is that the God who creates is the God who redeems, and that Christ is the organ, or medium, of His action in both realms. In a glorious sentence that we owe to the learned Dr. Lightfoot, "The Eternal Word is the goal of the universe as He was the starting-point. It must end in unity, as it proceeded from unity: and the center of this unity is Christ."

This eternal, creating Christ, whom Paul worshipped and proclaimed as Saviour, became the historic Jesus. Verse 22 speaks of "the body of his flesh." The error-peddlers in Colossae were teaching otherwise. They compounded their heresy by holding, first, that matter is impure, and second, that therefore it would degrade Christ for Him to be identified with a physical body. All of it bad philosophy and worse religion, in our apostle's view.

Paul, on the contrary, would have applauded Charles Wesley's lines, sung by millions every Christmas:

> "Late in time behold Him come,
> Offspring of a virgin's womb.
> Veiled in flesh the Godhead see,
> Hail the incarnate Deity!"

Christ the Creator eternal! Christ the incarnate Word historical! It is He, cries Paul, who is Christ the atoning Saviour universal. In reading this chapter I suggest that you do a mental "hold" after verse 14 until you reach verse 20. Thus: "In whom we have redemption through his blood, even the forgiveness of sins. . . . And having made peace through the blood of his cross, by him to reconcile all things unto himself."

J. S. Stewart has a moving passage in one of his books, in which he quotes Huxley, saying "There is no such thing as forgiveness," and Bernard Shaw, saying "Forgiveness is a beggar's refuge, we must pay our debts," and H. G. Wells, saying that the ultimate power is never forgiving but is "a harsh implacable hostility." To all of which, says Stewart, we Christians can reply, "Thanks for the information, but it is not your hidebound logic, it is heaven's grace that reigns!"

He might have added — as indeed he does in many another passage — that it reigns from the Cross!

> "O Christ, love's victim hanging high
>   Upon the cruel Tree,
> What worthy recompense can I
>   Make, mine own Christ, to Thee?
> My sweat and labor from this day,
>   My sole life, let it be,
> To love Thee aye the best I may
>   And die for love of Thee."

But if the *heart* of Paul's message is Christ as Saviour and Lord, it was not the *whole* of his message. Christ for the world? Yes. But Christ for the Church — the Christians — also! Here the apostle proclaims Him as *Teacher* and *Example*. Take, for instance, the plea and directive he gives in Chapter 2, verses 6 and 7: "As ye have therefore received Christ Jesus the Lord, so walk ye in him; rooted and built up in him, and established in the faith, as ye have been taught, abounding therein with thanksgiving."

Had not Jesus said "I have given you an example"? Had He not insisted, "If ye know these things, happy are ye if ye do them"?

And these words of His must be taken, not too woodenly, but elastically — under the guidance of the Holy Spirit. After all, there is a narrow sense in which our Lord did *not* give us an example of all modes of Christian behavior. We search His life in vain for any example of how a husband is to behave towards his wife. Millions have drawn inspiration from Thomas à Kempis' *The Imitation of Christ* and Charles Sheldon's *In His Steps,* but either one of them is capable of misleading us. The climate of the *Imitation* is one in which the *ideal* life is really monastic; and as for *In His Steps,* there are many life-situations in which you and I must ask, not precisely "What would Jesus do?" but "What would Jesus have me do here and now?"

To cite cases, it was a mistake for the Christian slaveholders of Britain and the United States to be complacent about human slavery and to justify their complacency by the fact that neither Jesus nor Paul openly attacked the slave system in the Roman Empire. What Christians could, and should do, as a minority in a pagan police state, and what they can and should do in a free society which professes to be Christian are two different things. It was the piercing of the social conscience by the light of Christ's mind that finally tore slavery from the fabric of our society.

A similar situation exists today — over *race* and *civil rights.* In one of the unhappiest interludes in the church's history in the United States millions of our members pay more heed to a rooted social custom than to a conscience shot through wtih the Master's passion for justice. Let us not forget that it was a church which had lost its "savor" — inner spiritual vitality and outer social witness — that was "cast out" and "trodden under foot of men" in the Communist's revolution of 1917.

"Learn of me" said Jesus — learn what I burningly felt that day I took hold of the "money changers" (the representatives of entrenched exploitation) and drove them from the temple.

If the message of Christ as Saviour and Lord gives us our *evangel,* the message of Christ as Teacher and Example gives us our *ethic.*

Both are needed. Neither must be left out.

B. There is something else we must get hold of in our text. We have been saying that Paul's was the message of a Person. We must now go on to say that it was the message of a *Possession.* What does it mean for this man to say that he has been commissioned to proclaim "Christ *in* you?"

I do not forget that the preposition in the Greek will permit the translation "among you." Moffatt renders it that way. But he stands pretty much alone. Because "in you" is so thoroughly true to Paul's familiar doctrine of our "union with Christ" — Christ in us and we in Christ — we are safe in going along with the overwhelming majority of translators.

But the point here is far more than technical. "Christ *in* you" means Christ personally experienced and assuredly known.

We must realize that there are many areas of reality in which Jesus Christ is firmly rooted: history, theology, morals, liturgy, sacraments, and so on.

Christ in *history?* Yes, but this of which Paul is speaking is more.

Christ in *theology?* Yes, but this is more.

Christ in *ethics and ideals?* Yes, but this is more.

Christ in *architecture, poetry, liturgy?* Yes, but this is more.

Christ in *you!*

Is He *there?* With your consent? Through your faith? To your knowledge?

I recall reading, years ago, about a peasant couple in France who were visited by a godly priest. The husband was out at the moment. When he returned, his wife said, "The priest came to see us."

"What did he say?"

"He asked if Jesus Christ lived here."

"Did you tell him we belong to the church?"

"That isn't what he asked. He wanted to know if Jesus Christ lives here."

That's *different!*

Is it not fair to ask: How would *you* have answered?

> "O live in us this day,
>   O clothe Thyself, Thy purpose yet again
> In human clay:
>   Work through our feebleness Thy strength,
>   Work through our meanness Thy nobility,
>   Work through our helpless poverty of soul
>   Thy grace, Thy glory, and Thy love."

"O live *in us* this day."

There *is* an answer to that prayer.

C. One thing more about the message: it is the message of a *Prospect.* "Christ in you" says Paul, is "the hope of glory."

Glory is a Biblical word that flashes with a hundred colors. It has many shades of meaning in many forms of expression. In general, it is the active and radiant presence of God in holiness, majesty, and, if one may so couch it, in *fulfillment of purpose.* Thus the death and resurrection of Jesus can be described as the *glorifying* of the Son of man: the fulfillment of the Father's purpose in Him and of His purpose in the Father.

Now it was an essential part of the revelation given to the apostles that it was in the purpose of God, in Christ, to bring to final completion the victory over all the dark and destructive forces of the world which had been decisively won on the cross and through the resurrection. This would mean, in the end, a re-appearing of Christ, a Second Advent, an overthrowing of death, an ending of all the grimness and gloom whose dark symbol is the grave, a smashing of the last stubborn relic of that mortality which has so often been the occasion, if not the cause, of shattered health, nagging fears, faded dreams, misted vision, and threatened sanctity.

This purpose of the sovereign God, cries Paul, warranted and winged by the resurrection of Christ, will be invincibly fulfilled. Therein lies your hope.

A horde of Bertrand Russells may bitterly pronounce, "Brief and powerless is man's life. On him and all his race the sure, slow doom falls pitiless and dark."

But that is a stance they *choose* to take. Declining to choose Christ, this is the position they must take.

But no such despairing cynicism ever seized the soul of a Christian. His is the unshakable hope that sings:

"Faith will outlast the bitter hour,
Hope will outshine the darkest fear,
Love will outmatch the strongest power
That threatens all the soul holds dear —

"For Faith will conquer, Hope abide,
And Love will reign the Throne beside,
When sin, and fear, and death, have died."

The Person! The Possession! The Prospect!

It is all there in my message, cries Paul. The truth of it lives in my heart and the telling of it leaps from my lips. Whether by "warning" or by "teaching" — and always in the strength of that divine power which "worketh in me mightily" — I live to make this message known.

Who steps forward to join the Pauline partnership?

Colossians 2

THE AGONY AND ECSTASY OF CARING

2:1. "For I would that ye knew what great conflict [mar-gin, 'care'], I have for you."

I. HISTORICAL SETTING. In this chapter Paul will de-liver his "polemic," as some New Testament scholars put it, against the teachers of the "Colossian heresy" previously re-ferred to in our notes. Starting with verse 8 is a series of references to "any man" and "no man" which, because of Paul's use of the singular form, may be taken (and by a number of expositors *is* taken) to mean a particular teacher who was pershaps the chief exponent of these false and dan-gerous views.

II. EXPOSITORY MEANING
   2:1. "Conflict." Strong in the Greek; it is the word from which we derive "agonize" and "agony."
   2:2. "Comforted," in this context, is better rendered "strengthened," or "encouraged." (Weymouth uses "cheered" and the New English Bible "good heart.") The whole clause, "the acknowledgment of the mystery of God, and of the Father, and of Christ," makes tough going both for trans-lators and expositors: for *translators* because of the extraor-dinary diversity of manuscript readings, for *expositors* be-cause the shade of theological meaning differs slightly ac-cording to the particular reading that is chosen. There is good reason for commending the rendering of the Revised Standard Version, which reads simply, "the knowledge of God's mystery, of Christ," thus placing "of Christ" in apposi-tion with the mystery.
   2:5. "Order." Your orderly condition, as of an army that has not broken ranks.

2:8. "Philosophy." Used nowhere else in Scripture, the context here would suggest that it should be set in quotation marks; that is to say, *so-called* philosophy. What the Colossian errorists would dignify as philosophy Paul would debunk as "vain deceit," that is, something delusively speculative.

"Rudiments of the world" may be understood as referring (1) to rites and ordinances (perhaps Jewish), or (2) to heavenly bodies or natural forces personified, or (3) to Paul's judgment that the errorists are presenting something which they wish to have accepted as spiritual when in fact it is nothing but "ABC's" offered on a natural, or worldly, level.

2:9. "Bodily" should be taken to mean "in bodily wise" (Robertson), or "with a bodily manifestation" (Lightfoot).

2:10. "Complete in Him" is rendered in the Revised Standard Version "You have come to fulness of life in him"; and Moule, after giving us the translation, "You are filled full in Him in whom resides all fulness," gives us this dilation: "In His promise, presence, power, you do possess 'all things needful for life and godliness.' "

2:11. "Of the sins" should be omitted as being without sufficient manuscript authority.

By "the body of the flesh" (taking the phrase as amended) is meant something typically Pauline: not the physical body but the totality of the self-life, human nature apart from the renewing, purifying grace of God. This interpretation, at any rate, seems most consonant with Paul's distinctive, *ethical* use of "flesh," though it must not be forgotten that in some passages he employs it in obvious reference to the physical body.

2:12. "Buried with him in baptism." Despite the *majority* opinion of commentators, the view of such a careful expositor as Bishop Nicholson should not be dismissed out of hand, namely, that Paul is here using "baptism" in the nonceremonial sense in which Jesus used it when He said, in reference to His death, "I have a baptism to be baptized with" (Luke 12:50). Nicholson concludes that the meaning of Paul's words is best understood in light of such a passage as I Corinthians 12:13. It scarcely need be added that such a view does not carry with it the unwarranted extreme of ultra-dispensationalism in its insistence that water-baptism has been done away.

2:14. "The handwriting of ordinances." "The Mosaic law, which being unfulfilled is analogous to an unpaid 'note of hand' " (Abbott). Not that the law of God is regarded as an evil to be abolished, but that it is here portrayed, owing to its claims against the violator, as an enemy, a hostility, making our salvation and peace impossible. *That* predicament the cross has dealt with, overcome, cancelled out.

2:15. "Having spoiled principalities and powers." Christ took the whole hierarchy of evil (personal or impersonal) and despoiled it, stripped it of power as a conqueror strips spoils from his vanquished foe.

2:16. "Judge" may be understood in an adverse sense: "judge against you." In "holyday," "new moon," and "sabbath" three kinds of feasts in the Jewish calendar may be seen: annual, monthly, and weekly.

2:17. "Body" is to be understood as "substance," solid and enduring *reality*.

2:18. "Beguile you of your reward." One word in Greek, and whether it implies the idea of a "reward," or "prize," is an issue on which scholars are divided. What is clear is the thought of *disqualification*.

"Voluntary humility." A knotty phrase, subject of endless discussion, which is perhaps best rendered, "of his own mere will, by humility." Grammatically it may be regarded as modifying either the would-be disqualifier or the one whose disqualification is being attempted. In either case "humility" denotes a self-assumed and therefore artificial humility.

"Intruding into those things which he hath not seen." On good manuscript authority the negative may be omitted and the whole phrase interpreted ironically, as "busying himself with his 'visions.' "

2:19. "Not holding the Head." Excellently rendered in the Revised Standard Version, "not holding fast to the Head."

2:20. "Rudiments of the world." Either the "Jewish ceremonials" which were, comparatively, earthy, unspiritual (so Erdman) or perhaps with the errorists especially in mind, the angels, aeons, personified astral forces, of which they made so much.

"Ordinances." Required ceremonies and ascetic practices, already alluded to in verse 16.

2:21, 22. The parenthesis is a kind of watchword summary of prohibitions, a taboo scheme, so to speak, which was thought to have saving merit.

2:23. "A show of wisdom" means a *pretension* to wisdom.

"Will worship." A self-conscious and self-confident voluntarism far removed from humble trust in Christ; if a paraphrase is desired, the New English Bible's reading of "forced piety" is excellent.

"Neglecting of the body." Literally, *treating it unsparingly*, that is, by ascetic impositions and denials.

"Not in any honor to the satisfying of the flesh," is well altered by Moule into "not of any value against the indulgence of the flesh."

III. DOCTRINAL VALUE. As against the false doctrine (propagated by the Colossian errorists) of emanations and aeons, quasi-deities that perform a variety of services, including the creation of the material order, this chapter urges the full deity and sovereignty of Jesus Christ, who is the open secret and the perfect summing up of God. He is the "mystery" of God laid open; He is the "fulness" of God unveiled. Moreover, as against a scheme of grace-works (which means grace corrupted) Paul expounds his doctrine of the believer's faith-union with Christ, who alone is sufficient for the *living* of the saved life, as He was alone sufficient for the *provision* of this salvation on the cross.

IV. PRACTICAL AIM. It is in this chapter that Paul is most explicit in his handling of the "Colossian heresy," though he refrains from naming its ringleader. His purpose is to arm the church against errors that detract from Christ's unshared honor as Creator and Saviour and that compromise the whole stucture of salvation as the gift of God in Christ through grace.

V. HOMILETICAL FORM

Theme: "The Agony and Ecstasy of Caring."

Introduction: Writing on the deeper meaning of sympathy — the ability to put oneself in the other person's place — Walt Whitman has some pungent lines in which he says:

> "Agonies are one of my changes of garments.
> I do not ask the wounded person how he feels.
> I myself become the wounded person."

It was like this with Paul. He could say, in a dimension of meaning far deeper than Whitman could comprehend: "Agonies are one of my changes of garments."

"I would that ye knew what great conflict I have for you." The marginal reading of the Authorized Version is better. It gives us the word "care" in place of "conflict." "Deep concern" is the Moffatt rendering, while Phillips has it "anxiety." "Strenuous exertions" is the paraphrase of the New English Bible.

Whatever the translation, the Greek word is none other than the one from which we derive "agony" and "agonize." No shallow pin-prick is this that the apostle feels. It has depth and acuteness.

A. The meaning of the *pain that Paul feels.* I see at least three things in it:

There is *affection* in it.

In the opening of the letter he has commended the Colossians for what he calls "the love ye have to all the saints" (1:4). Within that circle of affection, we may be sure, this man Paul has his place. If *they* loved all the saints, *he* was not a whit behind.

The more we are ruled by the love of Christ the more care we feel for people. And let it be added, for people *as persons.* Not as *things* to be used, nor as *agents* to be employed, nor as *prospects* to be "sold," but as *persons* to be served for their own sake and for Christ's.

But what if they do not want our service, or our care, or our love? What if, indeed, they strike back at us with resentment, or bitterness, or hatred?

Or, to state the matter in less ugly form, what if they are not even aware that they need our love and help?

Do we withhold love? No. Or, worse still, do we replace it with a bitterness that we hurl back at those who are bitter towards us? Never.

This is part of love's pain. It is prepared to take risks. It is willing to get hurt. It imposes no conditions and asks no reward.

It was said of Mrs. Catherine Booth, moving amid the shadows and the squalor of London's East End, that she "could not see a neglected sore or witness a ruthless wrong without a pain that sometimes became physical nausea."

Love cares. Because it cares, it suffers.

I see something else in Paul's pain.

There was *alarm* in it.

Let me remind you of an incident in Paul's life, the portrayal of which has often reappeared on the screen of my mind — always hauntingly, disturbingly. It is recorded in the 20th chapter of the Book of Acts. Paul has asked the elders of the Church at Ephesus to come down to the seaport at Miletus and meet with him while his ship is in harbor. It is the last time that he will ever see them, and he knows it. He speaks tenderly but gravely. "Remember," he says, going back to the time he was their minister, "that by the space of three years I ceased not to warn every one night and day with tears" (v. 31).

Then, scanning the future, he pleads: "Take heed therefore unto yourselves, and to all the flock, over which the Holy Ghost hath made you overseers.... For I know this, that after my departing shall grievous wolves enter in among you, not sparing the flock" (vv. 28, 29).

Wolves did prey upon that Ephesian congregation, in the midst of which the apostle had labored with unflagging zeal.

But here, at Colossae, was a Christian community that Paul had never seen, it seems. Nevertheless, they are his

Christian brothers and sisters. And the wolves are after them. The errorists are trying cunningly to divide their loyalties between Christ and ceremonialism, between Christ and astrology, and between Christ and asceticism.

Paul is alarmed. He knows full well that a divided Christ is a dishonored Christ. He must therefore warn them.

"Were the highest heavens my pulpit," cried one of the early Church Fathers, "and the whole host of the redeemed my audience, Jesus alone would be my text." When we see members of our church, or of our Sunday School class, or of our family, drifting away from *that,* there is good reason for us to be alarmed.

Small wonder, then, that Paul should say, to put the text in the Phillips translation, "I wish you could understand how deep is my anxiety for you."

I see a third thing in Paul's pain.

There is *action* in it.

Affection and alarm, if not overtly and constructively expressed, can be pathetically negative. They can tie us up in knots, make us red-faced with anger, or enervate us with self-pity. The last of these effects is a psychological twist in which we feel sorry for ourselves that *we* should have to care so much, that we should be required to feel so deeply.

Paul never fell into this trap. Even though he was a prisoner, he did something. His affection found an outlet, his alarm got hold of a vehicle.

For one thing, Paul *acted* in prayer. We "do not cease to pray for you," he assures them (1:9). Although the word "prayer" does not appear in our text, many students of this passage see a reference to it in Paul's use of the Greek word whence "agony" comes.

Many of us know something of the *nestling* side of prayer — sweet, comforting, nourishing communion with God. But few of us are acquainted with the *wrestling* side of prayer — lining up with God in holy combat against the dark, destructive forces that are loose in the world. One of Britain's noblest spiritual shepherds was John Welsh, who at times would tarry so far into the night in private intercessions that his wife would call to him, bowed there in the manse with only a plaid flung around his shoulders, telling him that he must get his sleep. He once replied, "Oh, woman, I have the souls of three thousand to answer for, and I know not how it is with many of them."

Quite honestly, how long has it been since the passion and heat of your caring drove *you* to your knees, there to join with God in His concern for someone far from light, or deep in sorrow, or shackled by evil? When was the last time — if ever — there were any tears to give a holy saturation to your prayers?

Paul acted in another way.

He wrote a letter. He could not go to his Colossian friends in person, for he was Caesar's prisoner. He could not send them a telegram, for there were no cable services. He did what he could. And this Epistle was the result. Into every sentence of it he packed his heart. Upon its parchment he dropped his tears. In passage after passage of it he bared his soul and gave his witness.

John Wesley, on one of his visits to Ireland, met a young lady who was not in good health. What weighed the more on Wesley's mind was that she had never given her heart to Christ. He later wrote a letter. The busy, but now elderly, man poured out his soul to her: "Believe me, my dear maid, what are called pleasures and diversions can give you no solid happiness. They are poor, empty, insignificant trifles. . . . You were made a little lower than the angels, that you might live with them forever. You are come forth from God, and are returning to God, as fast as a few fleeting years can carry you. But I am in pain for you; I am concerned lest you should forget this, like other pretty, giddy, unthinking creatures. . . . O make haste. Be a Christian, a real Bible Christian now!"

"I am in pain for you!"

And Wesley *did* something about it.

But if caring for people is often expensive in the coin of pain, we must see that, fully as often, it has its brighter, rewarding side.

B. Note *the pleasure Paul tastes*. Look at verse 5, reading it in a vernacular translation such as Moffatt's: "although I am absent in body, I am with you in spirit, and it is a joy to note your steadiness and the solid front of your faith in Christ."

The report that Epaphras had brought to Paul from Colossae was not all a tale of woe. It had in it many a good reason for rejoicing. Grave dangers hung over the church but, for the most part, the believers were steadfast in their faith, firm in their loyalty.

In these Christians Paul has discovered a dual loyalty. On the one hand, there was a *corporate* loyalty which had kept them related and united to one another. This was their "order," or "orderliness," and it contrasted pleasantly with the disorder and division that marred that church at Corinth.

On the other hand, there was the *personal* loyalty that they have given, in faith, to Jesus Christ.

On both counts Paul's heart is happy. His concern for them being as intense as it is — and this despite the fact that he has never seen their faces — no victory of theirs can be won, no fine thing about them can be evident, without its cheering his heart and gladdening his day.

It is this sort of care for people that is in short supply in these lonely, grubby, hectic days through which millions of us are passing. What is wanted is care that is eager, hopeful, outgoing, imaginative, and grateful. By those who are strangers to the Christian faith it is needed to nourish within them a sense of significance, of hope, of being wanted and welcomed. By those of us who profess faith it is needed to prevent our own souls from shriveling down to the size of our pay-check or the bed in which we comfortably lie.

> "Neither moteless nor beamless,
> But sightless the eye
> That sees things and not people."

It was the pleasure of caring, as well as its pain, that flowed out so picturesquely in those words of Samuel Rutherford's, descriptive of his feeling toward his congregation: "My witness is above that your heaven would be two heavens to me,

and the salvation of you all as two salvations to me. I would
agree to a suspension and postponement of my heaven for
many hundreds of years, if ye could so be assured of a lodging
in my Father's house."

And cut from the same fine bolt of silk are the verses of
some (to me) unknown poet who wrote:

> "And up the radiant peopled way
>   That opens into worlds unknown
> It will be life's delight to say,
>   'Heaven is not heaven for me alone.'
>
> "Rich by my brother's poverty? —
>   Such wealth were worthless! I am blest
> Only in what they share with me,
>   In what I share with all the rest."

C. *Finally there is the progress which Paul asks.*

The apostle's caring has a *goal*. The twinge of pain and
the taste of pleasure have alike a target of progress. To describe it, in Paul's case, we need note verses 2 and 6 in the
context. Let us take Barclay's translation of verse 2: "My
struggle is that their hearts may be encouraged, that they may
be united together in love, that they may come to all the
wealth of the assured ability to make the right decision in
any situation, to the knowledge of that truth which only
God's own may know, I mean of Christ, in whom are hidden
all the treasures of wisdom and knowledge."

Put quite simply, Paul longs that these distant friends of
his may, first of all, experience *love's enrichment*. Before he
is finished with this letter, he will tell them that "love is the
bond of perfectness," or the "perfect girdle," as one translation has it. It is the strengthening of that bond for which he
is praying.

Note the force of "knit together." It is in *community* that
love grows, even as it is by *love* that community is cemented.

Love's growth, however, is more than a progressive en-
hancement of the sense of togetherness. It is a progressive
enlightenment in the verities and values that are all summed
up in Christ. It is in the *knowing* of Christ that we find the
key to "the right decision in any situation."

No one knew better than Paul the importance of this link between love and knowledge. His desire for the Colossians was the same as that which he cherished for the Philippians: "This I pray, that your love may abound yet more and more in knowledge and in all judgment" (1:9). As faith without works is dead, love without knowledge is blind.

George Washington Carver was a young Christian at Simpson College in Iowa. He was interested in becoming a painter. One day a teacher whom he greatly respected said to him, "George, what your people need is improved agriculture." Carver listened, impressed by the facts that were presented. There and then his life "call" took shape within him. His artist's paraphernalia went to the bottom of his trunk. Out of care for the South and its poorer people, Negro and white, he began to study agriculture. The career that later unfolded is easily one of the finest in our American tradition. From the sweet potato he extracted 150 commercial products, and from the unpretentious peanut he drew 300! It is said that he added 50 million dollars to the agriculture of the South. Into how many lives he brought some relief from the burden of poverty or near-poverty no one knows.

What one does know is that love for God and love for people lay behind Carver's caring.

Now take verse 6; "So, then, as you have received Christ, Jesus the Lord, live your life in Him," or, "so go on living in Him," as Phillips has it.

So the target of Paul's concern for these Christians is, first, love's enrichment, and, secondly, *life's advancement.*

Actually, in order to make vivid the growth aspect of the Christian life the apostle puts together in swift succession three dynamic metaphors: a man, a tree, and a building. The man is *walking,* the tree is *growing,* and the building is *rising.*

Out of the throbbing heart of this imprisoned man comes the expressed longing:

I want you to walk in Christ!
I want you to be rooted in Christ!
I want you to be built up in Christ!

So speaks the soul in which love's concern, love's caring —
both its agony and its ecstasy — are at work.

What about it with you — and me? As those who call themselves the friends of Christ, are we similarly exercised? Do
we care?

If so, and if it be love's solicitude that moves us, there is
scarcely any limit to what God can do through us — minister-
ing to others.

It is told of Richard Baxter's congregation that its members would sometimes say, "We take all things well from one
who always and wholly loves us."

Who *cares*?

Colossians 3

MANDATE FOR GRATITUDE

3:15. "And be ye thankful."

I. HISTORICAL SETTING. Historically, this chapter must be read against a threefold backdrop: (1) the morals of a community such as Phrygian Colossae (vv. 5-9); (2) the racial and cultural exclusiveness of the time (v. 12); and (3) the domestic and economic situation by which the Roman Empire was characterized (vv. 18-25).

II. EXPOSITORY MEANING

3:1. "If" has the force of "since," pointing not to uncertainy but to logical causality.

"Be risen." More correctly rendered, "you were raised," to bring out the decisive past action required by the Greek aorist. The principle of *identification,* introduced in the preceding chapter, is carried forward, but now with particular reference to its implications. The three facets of the principle are: (1) in a historical sense, we died and were raised when Christ died and arose; (2) in principle we died and rose again when by faith we received Him as our Life and Lord, our Saviour and Sanctifier; (3) in practical experience we are enabled to apply the principle of identification and to live in the power of His risen life, but only as we clearly see our position and privilege in Him and allow Him, by the Holy Spirit, to make the principle *operational* across the entire spectrum of our living.

3:2. "Affection" is better rendered "mind," the meaning being "let this be the disposition and bent of your thoughts and desires." If the indicatives of this opening paragraph (vv. 1-4) are important, so are the imperatives. In logical se-

quence, the indicatives are: "You have died" (v. 3.), "you
have been raised" (v. 1), "your life is hid with Christ" (v.
3). Thus the Revised Standard Version. The imperatives are:
"put to death . . . what is earthly in you" (v. 5), "seek the
things that are above" (v. 1), "set your mind on things that
are above" (v. 2). In the indicatives we have a set of *facts*
which God in Christ has established; in the imperatives we
have a series of *functions* in which our faith is to be con-
tinuously engaged.

3:4. In this verse the distinction is between the indicative
and the predicative: "Christ . . . *is* our life"; you *"will* appear
with Him in glory" (RSV).

3:5. "Mortify." Not "deaden," as some late versions have it,
but "make dead," which is a Greek aorist imperative.

"Members." That is, *parts* or *faculties,* whether of the body
or of the mind.

"Which are upon the earth." Related, that is, to your
practical, earthly life, as distinguished from your true, or
heavenly life, which is "Christ in you." Since you have died,
your old, independent ego having been consigned to the
place of death — the cross — settle it now, once for all, that
the principle of death must govern the functioning and use
of every instinct and drive, every appetite and temper, of
your whole being. Living by the Christian death-principle is
streets removed from living by the ascetic schemes of the
Colossian errorists. For them, the mortal, or physical side of
man's being, is inherently evil, a defilement and a degrada-
tion. For enlightened Christians neither the body nor its
instinctual drives — gregariousness, sexuality, aggressiveness —
can properly be called sinful. It is the perversion and distor-
tion of these capacities that is sinful and this springs from the
sinfully infected ego. Etymology and theology can sometimes
curiously clash. Etymologically, to have a body is to be
"carnal." But Paul never uses "carnal" in this sense. He uses
it in the sense of being "carnally *minded,"* which is very
different. To be "carnally minded" is a disposition to put the
rule of appetite or ambition above the rule of Christ. It is

this disposition that must drop its proud head at Calvary and say, "finished."

In this verse Paul makes a swift shift from the thought of capacities to the use — in this case the *wrong* use — of those capacities. The results: "fornication, indecency, lust, foul cravings, and the ruthless greed which is nothing less than idolatry" (NEB).

3:8. "Put off." Another aorist imperative, meaning definitely and completely.

"Anger" and "wrath" are distinguished from one another as sullen, persistent bad temper is distinguished from sudden outbursts.

"Malice" is well rendered "ill will" by Weymouth.

3:9. "The old man." In Pauline usage it appears to be a more inclusive expression than such expressions as "sin that dwelleth in me," "carnally minded," and "flesh." It is the totality of what we are apart from Christ and His saving offices.

3:10. "The new man." From one point of view the "new man" is Christ, since, as Paul expresses it elsewhere, *He* is "made unto us wisdom, and righteousness, and sanctification, and redemption" (I Cor. 1:30); from another point of view the "new man" is individually the "new creature," or "new creation" (II Cor. 5:17); and, from yet another point of view, the "new man" is corporately the *new community,* the *new collectivity,* the *church* (Eph. 2:15). All three are probably in Paul's mind as he writes this sentence, though the first two meanings would seem to be most prominent.

In all of these "aorists" there are implications of utmost importance. Too many commentators ignore them or treat them slightly. It is not too much to say that the whole dialectic of New Testament sanctification is involved. Paul is assuring the Colossian believers that provisionally, when Christ died, and positionally, when they by faith came into Christ and He into them, all this became true: they died and rose again, they "put off the old man" and they "put on the new." Or, to use terms which appear elsewhere in the Pauline writings, their sanctification, no less than their justification,

was complete. It could not be otherwise if God has made
Christ the "righteousness" and "sanctification" of all believers.

And yet much of the whole burden of what Paul says in
this section of the Epistle may be described thus: Brothers,
you are not in experiential fact what you are in spiritual
position and privilege. And you never will be, no matter how
many years you struggle along, until you see what your union
with Christ really means, until you let this identification-
principle become operational in you, until, that is, you begin
to *realize* that victory and sanctity are never the end-result of
your trying, or straining, or even your asking for Christ to
step in and give you some *help,* but rather the consequence
of your letting Christ *take over,* letting Him be in fact Christ
in you living out His life in your always impotent and unworthy but unreservedly yielded being.

It is by way of discerning comment on this very passage in
Colossians that Bishop Handley Moule speaks of these believers as having indeed put on "the new man," but "this was
a matter of position and of possession. There must also be
the 'putting on' of *realization,* and of *use,* and of *manifestation*; or the blessed means will miss its end."

Reading such a book as Gilchrist Lawson's *The Deeper
Experiences of Famous Christians,* one is made aware of how
crucial the day or the hour of this "realization" can be.

As for the on-going process of sanctification, it is clearly
recognized by Paul in the clause which modifies the phrase
"the new man": "which is renewed in knowledge after the
image of him that created him." The present participle
should be translated "is being renewed," or, amplified, "is
being ever renewed." In deeper, richer personal knowledge of
Christ the new man is being assimilated more and more to
the likeness of the Creator-God who has been faultlessly revealed in Christ the Son.

3:11. "Where." In the region and at the level of "the new
man." And now the stress falls more heavily on the corporate,
or communal, character of the new entity — the society of the
twice-born. Here, where "Christ is all," the dividing barriers

are all down: racial ("Greek nor Jew") ceremonial ("circumcision nor uncircumcision"), lingual-cultural ("Barbarian, Scythian"), social ("bond nor free").

3:12. "Bowels of mercies" is well paraphrased "a heart of compassion."

3:14. "Charity." Love.

"The bond of perfectness." That is, it is the perfect bond, or girdle, binding all the virtues into a "harmonious whole."

3:15. "The peace of God." Good manuscript authority leads most later translators to adopt "the peace of Christ," thus giving us a reminder of John 14:27. It is the *assurance* and *serenity* which Christ Himself bestows.

"Rule." Literally, "act as umpire"; let it be *decisive, governing.*

"In one body." That is, "The unity of the Church belongs to your calling as Christians, not as something you are to achieve, but which you are to preserve"; therefore in conflicts of "motives or impulses or reasons" (the words are Lightfoot's) the "peace of Christ" must serve as referee or arbiter. It is impossible to do justice to Paul's thinking without giving to his phrase "in your hearts" a significance which, however personally real, is more than individualistic: it is communal.

3:16. "The word of Christ." A form of expression found only here in the New Testament; by many expositors it is taken to mean *the gospel* which, as an oral message, was in wide circulation during the period between the Lord's ascension and the time when the inspired documents were written and assembled. The gospel, it may be added, was more than the record of what our Lord *taught;* it was the narrative, the heralded announcement, of what our Lord *did* — the saving events of His death, burial, and resurrection.

"Dwell." That is "be at home in you, find a hospitality that is wide and worthy."

"In all wisdom." It is grammatically allowable and logically appropriate to attach this phrase to the participles that follow rather than to the verb that precedes; thus the Revised

Standard Version, "as you teach and admonish one another in all wisdom."

"Psalms and hymns and spiritual songs." Attempts to make precise distinctions between them are more or less arbitrary; Robertson suggests that the leading idea in "psalm" is that of the musical accompaniment, and in "hymn" it is that of praise to God, while "spiritual songs" is a general phrase which may be applied to either psalms or hymns, whether accompanied or unaccompanied.

3:18. "Submit yourselves." Phillips softens this to "adapt yourselves," which makes good sense, but takes too much liberty with Paul's words; Moule has it, "be loyal," which, though stronger, does not quite bring out the author's thought of the family as requiring a "head" and therefore requiring the recognition of that headship by the wife. The real softening of the word "submit," or "be subject," as several later versions have it, lies in two considerations: (1) the principle of *reciprocal* obligations on which Paul lays a heavy stress, something almost unknown in pagan society (where all the rights were the husband's), and too little known even in Jewish society, and (2) the fact that in Christian circles all inter-personal relations were to be treated as "in the Lord," that is, in the awareness that the whole of life comes under His eye, is to be lived as in His presence, and to be judged by His spirit.

3:21. "Provoke not." Meaning, "stop exasperating, or irritating." What is implied is a habitual nagging or over-severity which induces in some children excessive resistance but in others, perhaps most, an unhealthy regressiveness and dejection.

3:22. "According to the flesh" is taken to mean with *respect to outward, earthly relationships,* as distinguished from your higher relationship to the Lord.

"Eyeservice." Probably a Pauline coinage, which Moule renders "eye-bondage"; the modern counterpart of this kind of bond-servant is the office or factory employee who is a "clock-watcher."

3:24. "The reward of the inheritance." An eternal, heav-

enly inheritance by way of reward, is the meaning; abuses
of this perspective by those Christians who do, in effect, make
"religion the opiate of the people," must not be allowed
to wipe out future reward as a motivation (though by no
means the highest) for worthy service.

III. DOCTRINAL VALUE. In the opening paragraph of the
chapter the doctrine of the believer's (and the church's)
union with Christ, introduced earlier in the letter, is given
further exposition, but only as a kind of prelude to a discussion of its application in actual living.

IV. PRACTICAL AIM. Commencing with verse 5, Paul
shows how the Christian is to make the transition from *facts*
to the *functioning of facts,* from Christ as our death to sin to
Christ as our life in practical holiness. Beginning with verse
18, the target of the apostle's concern becomes the *home,*
where relationships between husband and wife, parent and
child, master and servant, are to be brought within the circle
of Christ's reigning lordship.

V. HOMILETICAL FORM

Theme: "Mandate for Gratitude."

Introduction: According to a medieval legend, two angels
were once sent down to earth, one to gather up the petitions
of men and women and the other to collect their thanksgivings. The first angel found petitions everywhere he went.
He returned to heaven with a load of them on his back and
a bundle of them in each hand. The second angel had no
such easy time with his assignment. He had to search dili-
gently and patiently for thanksgivings, and when at length
he went back to heaven he took with him a mere handful.

Legends, of course, can be far-fetched and fantastic or they
can be suggestively accurate. This one, we shall have to agree,
is much too accurate for comfort.

We are long on our demands, yes, even our complaints; we
are short on our thanksgivings.

But this we can say: it is no fault of the Apostle Paul's.
If the world had in it more people possessed of His spirit,

there would be no scarcity of praise.

Listen to the music of gratitude that plays through this Epistle alone:

First chapter, verse 3: *"We give thanks to God and the Father of our Lord Jesus Christ."*

First chapter, verse 12: *"giving thanks unto the Father."*

Second chapter, verse 7: *"abounding . . . with thanksgiving."*

Third chapter, verse 17: *"giving thanks unto God and the Father by Him"* (Christ).

Fourth chapter, verse 2: *"Continue in prayer, and watch in the same with thanksgiving."*

Wherever Paul went, he appeared in what one of the eloquent prophets calls "the garment of praise." There are some people, you well know, who, if they ever wear thankfulness at all, wear it as you do a boutonniere — on Mother's Day or at a wedding. But not Paul! He wore gratitude as a man wears his everyday suit. Praise was woven into the fabric of his life. He wanted it to be so with his Christian brethren everywhere. Hence this strong, imperative word of our text: "and be ye thankful."

A. Let us begin by facing it: gratitude is a *required* grace. Paul does not locate it among the luxuries of the Christian life; he gives it a place among the necessities.

See for yourself what company it keeps among the required rather than the elective courses in the college of Christian experience. Going back to verse 12, and using the Phillips translation, here are some commands of the Holy Spirit for you and me as members of the Christian community:

"Be merciful in action, kindly in heart, humble in mind."

Then verse 13: *"Be most patient and tolerant with one another, always ready to forgive if you have a difference with anyone."*

Verse 14: *"Be truly loving, for love is the golden chain of all the virtues."*

Then comes the first half of our text-verse: *"let the harmony of God reign in your hearts."*

Now, with no change in this imperative mood in which

the Apostle is writing, he says, as Phillips has it: *"never forget to be thankful for what God has done for you."*

How did so many of us come by the fanciful notion that gratitude is a matter of *emotion* and *inclination?* Christian thankfulness is far more a matter of *humility* and *duty.*

I owe it to *God* to be grateful: He has given me my being, my Saviour Christ, and my opportunity to do something with life other than whining about it or flinging it away.

I owe it to *others* to be thankful: a thankless, melancholy spirit spreads gloom, but a sunny, songful soul spreads a bracing contagion. It was said of that valiant, radiant missionary crusader, Francis Xavier, that if the brothers got discouraged it was sufficient to drive out the demon of depression if only they could go and look in his face.

And then I owe it to *myself* to be thankful: the meanness and sourness of ingratitude are injurious to good health, whereas thankfulness and praise have a healing and tonic effect.

Paul knew all of this. Because of it, he did not hesitate to rate thankfulness a required, and not merely a desirable, Christian trait.

B. Let us move on and say a second thing about gratitude: it is a *reasonable* grace. There are two reasons, it seems to me, why we may so describe it.

For one thing, it is reasonable because, on the lower, ordinary levels of life, it is just plain natural for us to *feel* gratitude. I say "feel" because an instinct of appreciation (often touched, I admit, with selfishness) asserts itself even in young children. In fact to *feel* gratitude is a much earlier experience than to *express* gratitude.

Here, for example, is a mother with her six-year-old son walking down the street in front of a church. A gentleman who knows the mother well stops to greet them. He pulls a nickel from his pocket and presents it to the little boy. The child's face lights up and his eyes sparkle with obvious appreciation. Yet no word of thanks crosses the child's lips. This will never do, the mother feels, so she says: "Johnny, say 'thank you' to the nice man." Not only did Johnny fail to respond, but the glow of gratitude went from his countenance and gave way to embarrassment and whimpering and even stubbornness. The lad was silent for no reason of ingratitude but because he was not accustomed to this sort of thing, especially where a stranger was in the act. The feeling was naturally there; the proper articulation of the feeling needed to be learned. For:

> "Hearts, like doors, will ope with ease
> To very, very little keys;
> And don't forget that two of these
> Are 'I thank you' and 'If you please.' "

But now, if we are going to dig into the more distinctively Christian teaching of Paul on gratitude, we must say a stronger thing. For this Apostle the reasonableness of thanksgiving has a firmer footing than its naturalness can ever give to it. He sees it as an attitude that Jesus Christ forms and fashions within the Christian soul. Thus we hear him say, in verse 17, *"Do all in the name of the Lord Jesus Christ, giving thanks unto God and the Father by him,"* or "through him," as other translations have it.

"Through *him!*"

If thankfulness arises through *prosperity,* well and good. Be sure to express it. But what are you going to do when the prosperity fails? You will then be tempted to feel that you have no *reason* to offer thanks.

If thankfulness springs up through *health,* well and good. You cannot be too expressive of your praise. But what will you do when accident maims you or disease makes you bedfast? Must you then become glum or bitter, feeling that you have no reason to sing a song of praise?

But now, supposing it is through our dear Lord Christ that you cultivate the fine art of thanksgiving, then what? The Christ, as Paul shows us in Chapter 1, through whom we "have redemption, even the forgiveness of sins!" The Christ through whom "we have peace through the blood of his cross!" The Christ through whom we have been "delivered from the power of darkness and translated into the kingdom" of the Son of God! The Christ through whom we are "strengthened with all might according to His glorious power unto all patience and long-suffering with joyfulness!"

Ah, this is different, is it not? For if it is *in Him* and *through Him* that I am to be a thankful soul, then money in the bank, however useful, does not have me at its mercy. If I lose it, I can still offer thanks. Then physical health, however great a boon, does not have me at its mercy; when it pales into disease or suffering, I can still be grateful.

A city missionary in London found a woman in the last stages of disease in a flat so grim and cold that poverty was written all over it. Yet the dying woman managed a faint smile as she said, "I have all I really need: I have Christ!"

Hearing which, someone wrote:

"In the heart of London city,
    'Mid the dwellings of the poor,
These bright golden words were uttered,
    'I have Christ.' What want I more?

"Spoken by a lonely woman,
    Dying on a garret floor,
Having not one earthly comfort —
    'I have Christ.' What want I more?

"He who heard them ran to fetch her
    Something from the world's great store;
It was needless — died she, saying
    'I have Christ!' What want I more?

"Oh, my dear, my fellow-sinner!
    High or low, or rich or poor,
Can you say with deep thanksgiving —
    'I have Christ!' What want I more?"

Make Christ the living fountain of your gratitude, and you will find that the requirement "Be ye thankful" is not unreasonable.

C. Following still another lead that our text gives us, let us say that gratitude is a *ripening* grace. The full meaning and measure of it does not come all in an instant. As the scholars frequently point out, if we were to translate the Apostle's words more literally, we should make the text read,

"And *become* ye thankful." Looking at it this way, we see that what Paul is really saying is this: "Brother Christians, I know you have the flower of gratitude planted in your hearts. But I want you to *cultivate* it. See to it that it grows."

Earlier in this letter Paul has used a phrase that must have moved them. In Chapter 2, verse 7, he speaks of *"abounding ...with thanksgiving."* Phillips takes that whole verse and draws it out in modern English thus: *"Grow out of Him as a plant grows out of the soil it is planted in, becoming more and more sure of your 'ground,' and your lives will overflow with joy and thankfulness."*

I doubt if any one ever really grows up in the business of thanksgiving unless he sees that gratitude is, more than anything else, an inner disposition towards life as a whole. Life has its heights and it has its valleys, its lights and its shadows, its glories and its glooms. That is the way it comes. It has been coming that way for a long time.

It is, therefore, our responsibility to decide where we are going to lay the emphasis, how we are going to evaluate things. William Park, to illustrate this, said to his students at Northfield, "Two girls gather grapes; one is happy because they have found the grapes and the other is unhappy because the grapes have seeds in them. Two women examine a bush; one is unhappy because it has thorns; the other notices the roses, and is overjoyed with their fragrance." Dr. Park added: *"We see exactly what we train ouselves to see in this life."*

Here is a man who, having been hale and husky for thirty years, gets a boil on the back of his neck and acts like a bear. You would think the whole universe had turned against him. Here is a woman — an actual case, by the way — who had been invalided and confined to her bed for many years. One day, when a friend came in to see her, she looked up and said, "Oh, I feel so happy and thankful!" When the visitor asked her why, she replied, *"Because the doctor tells me that if I continue to improve, and if the weather stays fine, and if nothing unusual happens, in two weeks I may be turned over and lie on the other side!"*

My friends, that comes only from a growing-up process in this grace of gratitude. That high quality of thankfulness comes only to someone who has learned that being grateful is not so much a matter of outward beatitude as it is a matter of inward attitude.

D. And finally, it should be seen that this required gratitude of which Paul speaks is a *rewarding* grace.

And it is this, I suggest, on three counts:

1. It *exalts* God. When man exalts himself, he succeeds only in being little and mean. When he exalts God, such is the paradox of it that he appears at his greatest and best.

That is a devastating word which Paul speaks in the opening chapter of Romans where, describing the wilful alienation of original man from God, he says, *"when they knew God, they glorified him not as God, neither were thankful"* (1:21).

Ingratitude is an insult to the Almighty. Thankfulness glorifies Him and, by mysterious reflex action, glorifies man.

2. But also, thanksgiving *expels gloom*. Look at the verse that follows our text: *"teach and help one another along the right road with your psalms and hymns and Christian songs, singing God's praises with joyful hearts"* (v. 16).

Some time ago I saw an intriguing title: "Gloomy Caesar and Happy Jesus." In the short article that followed, the author contrasted what we know of Tiberius Caesar, who ruled Rome in A.D. 30, with what we know of Jesus. Of Tiberius, with all his power and pomp and possessions, the historian Pliny wrote: "He is the gloomiest of mankind." But of Jesus we read that, sitting in the shadow of His Cross, He *"took bread, and gave thanks, and brake it, and gave it unto them"* (Luke 22:19). And when it was over, this holy supper, they sang "a hymn and went out" (Mark 14:26).

You and I are not to be the dispensers of Caesar's gloom; we are to be the transmitters of Jesus' joy!

3. And then, surely gratitude *encourages graciousness*. I like the way the Berkeley version translates the 6th verse of Chapter 4: *"Let your speech always be gracious."* I defy any-

one to achieve real graciousness without the conversational gift of saying "Thank you." If that is true at the social level, it is importantly true at the level of our relations with God.

Away then with whimpering! Away with the rasping voice of complaint and the jaundiced eye of fault-finding! Away with the rudeness that can find more things over which to be bitter than things over which to be blithe!

Thanksgiving is the politeness of the soul. Its reward may not be a million dollars. Its reward is a *gracious* spirit — and that's worth more than a million.

How movingly and delicately Adelaide Proctor has captured it in her lines called "Thankfulness":

> "My God, I thank Thee who hast made
>   The Earth so bright;
> So full of splendor and of joy,
>   Beauty and Light;
> So many glorious things are here,
>   Noble and right!

> "I thank Thee, too, that Thou hast made
>   Joy to abound;
> So many gentle thoughts and deeds
>   Circling us around
> That in the darkest spot of Earth
>   Some love is found.

> "I thank Thee more that all our joy
>   Is touched with pain;
> That shadows fall on brightest hours;
>   That thorns remain;
> So that Earth's bliss may be our guide,
>   And not our chain.

> "I thank Thee, Lord, that here our souls,
>   Though amply blest,
> Can never find, although they seek,
>   A perfect rest, —
> Nor ever shall, until they lean
>   On Jesus' breast!"

Colossians 4

HIS WILL AND OURS

4:12. "Stand perfect and complete in all the will of God."

I. HISTORICAL SETTING. (1) With respect to the conduct Paul urges, its context was that of the Christian community *vis-a-vis* pagan society; (2) with respect to Paul himself, he is seen as a prisoner in Rome, making personal comments about friends who stand in one relation or another to him and to the Colossians (e.g., Onesimus, the repentant run-away slave who is being returned to his master in Colossae) ; (3) with respect to the recipients of this letter, it is made clear that these were to include the congregation at Laodicea, another church in the Lycus Valley.

II. EXPOSITORY MEANING

4:1. "Just and equal." "Right and fair," the former suggesting *going by the rules,* the latter connoting *that which cannot be reduced to precise regulation.*

4:3. "Door of utterance." That is, an "open door for the Word of the gospel," neatly paraphrased in the New English Bible, "an opening for preaching."

"The mystery of Christ." To be understood in the light of 1:26-28. This "secret" of Christ, unlike those of the Colossian errorists, is an open secret, according to which Gentiles, no less than Jews, are included in Christ's redemption and have equal footing in Christ's Church. It was preaching this message that led to Paul's arrest and imprisonment.

4:5. "Them that are without." In the broad sense, all who are outside the circle of faith in Christ; in the narrower sense, the pagan neighbors of these Colossian believers.

4:6. "With grace." Meaning *graciousness.*

"Seasoned with salt." Characterized by a wholesome and savory liveliness.

"Know how ye ought to answer every man." The sense is well brought out in the New English Bible, "study how best to talk with each person you meet." Some people equate the saintly and the stodgy, and the pious and the prim. Paul never did. He believed that sanctity could sparkle and that winsomeness could make itself at home with godliness.

4:10. "Ye received commandments." These "orders" or "instructions" seem not to have been given by Paul, but by some other person or group, of which Paul had knowledge.

4:11. "Unto the kingdom of God." That is, *for,* or *in promotion of,* the kingdom of God.

4:12. "Laboring fervently." One word in Greek, meaning wrestling, struggling, and thus sharing in the same passionate ministry in which Paul was engaged, as we have seen in 2:1.

"Perfect." Several modern versions prefer "mature" (RSV, Moffatt, Berkeley, Phillips, for example). But the question, "In what sense?" has still to be faced. If readers of Paul think the use of "mature" as a synonym for "perfect" is a way to avoid difficulties of definition, they are mistaken. For example, let them try the substitution of the one for the other in the famous autobiographical passage in Philippians 3. "Not as though I . . . were already mature, but I follow after . . . ," he tells us in verse 12. But three verses later we find him saying, "Let us therefore, as many as be mature, be thus minded." The maturity of the non-mature is as much a paradox in Paul's teaching as if we were to call it the perfection of the imperfect. Nor does it honestly solve the problem to say, as some do, that in Christ we are fully mature and in ourselves we are always immature. Here is one of those false, because artificial, contrasts which do not arise out of the actual teaching of the apostle but, on the contrary, are imposed upon his teaching in our willingness to settle for explanations that do not explain. If all perfection, excepting God's, is relative, then it is possible that for Paul Christian maturity is a *stage* on the way, an enterable and verifiable stage, in the same sense (though these analogies are risky) as puberty is a stage on the way to adulthood, the adulthood (if we press this analogy) being thought of as the remoter, riper meaning of maturity. Confirmation of this view of Paul's dual teaching on perfection — this paradox of arrival and non-arrival, of the realized and yet-to-be realized — is found, it seems to me, in Ephesians 4:12-15, where "the mature man," he who has become the receiver of "the fulness of Christ," is not the finished man, the end-product in character of all God's chastening and ripening, but is simply the man who is no longer among the "children, tossed to and fro and carried about with every wind of doctrine." It is after this, and beyond this, that the "growing up" (v. 15) process goes on and on and on.

"Complete." Carries the meaning of "fully persuaded," or "fully assured."

4:15. "The church which is in his house." A difficult clause because of the variant manuscript readings; some have it "their house," raising the question whether this was *the* church in Laodicea or was one of two churches in the city. Lightfoot suggests that a family of Colossians had settled in Laodicea, and a company of believers was meeting there.

4:16. "The epistle from Laodicea." Four possibilities — (1) some lost letter of which we know nothing, (2) an extant letter called the "Epistle to the Laodiceans," called by Jerome in the fourth century a forgery, (3) the letter to Philemon, or (4) the letter to the Ephesians. Best assumption: that it was the letter we know as Ephesians, which was an encyclical. If this be correct, there would be an interchange between the churches of Colossae and Ephesus in which each would have the benefit of both letters.

III. DOCTRINAL VALUE. Theological considerations play only a minor role in this concluding chapter. There are implications in two areas: that of intercessory prayer and that of Christian sanctity.

IV. PRACTICAL AIM. This "practical" section of the letter comes to a close with *counsels, requests,* and *greetings*: the first having to do with such matters as master-slave relation-

ships and the manner in which Christians are to give their
witness before the pagans; the second, with such an expressed desire as Paul has for the faithful intercessions of his
friends as they pray or for encouragement to be given by
the Colossians to one of their office-bearers, Archippus; and
the third, with such salutations as those from their spiritual
father, Epaphras, and from Luke "the beloved physician."

V. HOMILETICAL FORM

Theme: "His Will and Ours."

Introduction: There are many ways to describe the wrongness, the brokenness, and the tragedy that are in the world.
One way is to speak of the whole unhappy confusion as a
clash of wills.

To be sure, it is partly a clash between the wills of human
beings. My will against yours! Yours against that trouble-
some neighbor's! His against his mother-in-law's! Hers against
the will of someone she is about to sue for damages! And on
and on it goes.

But if we are going to read life's realities deeply and
Christianly, we must see that the clash between human wills
is brought about because of a higher conflict — the clash between our wills and God's.

The man who is praying for these Colossians seems to
have in mind a picture of two circles. One circle represents
God's will for us and for our lives. The other represents our
own will. Move over from the circle of your self-will into the
circle of God's will, and stand there though the heavens fall!
This is what the prayer of Epaphras means. Between your
will and His there is to be not a *battling* but a *blending*.

Is this possible? Yes, though one does not say it is easy.
What does it mean?

A. Let us face it: *understanding God's will is our problem.*
When Paul learned that there were men and women in
Colossae who had but lately received Christ as their Saviour,
he wrote them: "Since the day we heard it," we "do not
cease to pray for you and to desire that ye might be filled

with the knowledge of his will in all wisdom and spiritual understanding." And why is this understanding of God's will important? For the best of reasons — a reason that is downright and earthy in its practicality: "That ye might walk worthy of the Lord unto all pleasing" (Col. 1:9, 10).

In an attempt to avoid — or to clear up — possible misunderstandings I want to make four suggestions:

1. It is important, I think, for us to realize that *our freedom of will is part of His will.* In creating human beings like ourselves He has willed, for His own purposes, that we should have wills, and that we should, within limits, exercise them freely.

Of course in doing this God took a risk. But it was a calculated risk. I have just said that it was for His own purpose that He endowed us humans with the power of choice. That purpose, the Bible makes clear, is this: that He might have a society of intelligent and morally responsible persons with whom He could have fellowship in a life of love and service. All this is gathered up, it seems to me, in one simple sentence recorded in Mark 3:14, where we are told that Jesus called the disciples "that they might be with him." That, in principle, is what lies behind creation. God wants fellowship; and fellowship, as someone has helpfully put it, is "a living intercourse between personalities."

But fellowship can never be forced. It can be asked for, sought, offered, but never coerced. The freedom to continue it or to break it off is always one of the conditions on which it rests. Any understanding of God's will must take this tremendous fact into account.

2. Our second remark is linked closely with the first: since our freedom of will is part of His will, *His will must sometimes be seen as a variable thing, while His character and His eternal purpose remain unchanged.*

Remember that human life, which was created as a *God*-centered thing, has become a *self*-centered thing. That is why Christian theology is so full of this word "salvation." There is a tragic "gone wrongness" about the human family. And God has to deal with it in judgment and mercy.

In this situation God's will as *intention* has to be distinguished from His will as *permission*.

For example, God's will as intention, as His real desire for us mortals on this earth, is that marriage should be the life companionship of one man with one woman. Nevertheless, when Jesus was compelled to face this problem of broken marriages, He remarked that under Moses it was permissible for a man to put away his wife for a variety of causes. But Jesus immediately added, "From the beginning it was not so." Divorce was allowed, as Jesus expressed it, because of the "hardness" of men's hearts. It was permitted while they were in a kindergarten stage of their moral development. Divorce is always, in one way or another, a testimony to human failure and folly. It is never God's intention.

Or, to cite another instance, God's will as intention is that human beings should be healthy. When He looked upon His original creation, the Bible tells us, He saw that it was "good." That means bodies glowing with health, minds functioning in harmony. But into the world of human perversity and folly has come a whole catalog of physical, emotional and mental ills. These are not God's desire — *that* were to make Him a fiend. But they are His permission, as part of the disciplinary order under which our lives must be lived as members of the sinful human family.

Applied to myself, this means that if I should come down tomorrow with a stroke of "polio," I shall not say that it was God's desire for me to be paralyzed, shrivelled in nerve and muscle, a threat to other people's health, and a burden to my family. My Christian faith will rather help me to say that, in a world of hazard such as this is, God has permitted me to suffer this stroke, and that even now He is working with me — whether by prayer or by medical skill and facility — to regain my health.

Within the framework of His will as permission there is a kind of interim purpose that He wants me to recognize. He wants me to pray that I may the better work with Him toward my recovery. He wants me to develop new habits of patience, new reaches of courage, new compassion for others, new insights into what values count for most.

Yes, and one thing more: He wants me to realize that what He is really working at, and one day will achieve victoriously, is a world in which these mortal ills will be swept clean away, and we shall have a fair land with no disease to wrack it, no graves to disfigure it.

3. Another point on which misunderstanding of God's will sometimes occurs is this: *His will for our character is permanently revealed in Christ, while His will for our career and the related details of our lives must be sought by each of us for himself.*

The Christian, Paul assures us, is predestined by God "to be conformed to the image of His Son" (Rom. 8:29). A man's first business is to receive Christ. With that, it is settled as to the *character* of the person he is to be. Christlikeness is the norm. He does not have to pray all night for a revelation of guidance as to whether he should be honest, though he may find occasion to pray for light on what exactly honesty means in a particular situation. He does not have to wait and wonder as to whether or not he should be loving, patient, courageous, loyal, generous, holy. The pattern has been set. The light has been given. We know. Christlike character is *always* God's will.

But not so with your *career* and mine. Am I to build houses or write books? Am I to be a farmer or an airplane pilot? Am I to be a minister's wife or an unmarried superintendent of nurses? Am I to master the piano or practice the unpopular craft of a watchmaker? In themselves the examples and teachings of Jesus give me no direct light on these questions. Here the will of God must be individualized. Each of us must seek it for himself; and seek it, let us add, in the confidence that, in one way or another, it will be given.

4. One further point on which we sometimes need help in understanding God's will is this: *we are not to conclude that if two courses are open to us, one of which is pleasant and the other unpleasant, the unpleasant one is necessarily His will.* Yet this is precisely the feeling that many people have.

One person concluded his conversation with a minister by saying, "Well, that is what I should like to do, so I thought it could not be the will of God."

Often it strikes me that the mood in which we say, "Thy will be done," in the Lord's Prayer is not at all the mood in which the Master intended us to utter those words. We repeat them, half dolefully, as if they represented nothing higher than an attitude of resignation. Why not think of them as words to be spoken joyously in the form of affirmation? You murmur, "Thy will be done," when you watch your darling wheeled up to the operating room for critical surgery. Why not say it radiantly when you hang up your children's Christmas stockings?

It is true, of course, that God's will may involve you in a course of action that is disagreeable to you, but my point is that the disagreeableness in itself is not the sign that it is His will. Wanting to be an electrical engineer may be just as truly a clue to His plan for you as your not wanting to be a missionary. The crucial point here is something that we shall grapple with at the end of this message.

B. Let us go on now to say that, if understanding God's will is our problem, *undertaking His will is our privilege.*

At the beginning of this letter that Paul wrote the Colossians *he* prayed, as we have seen, that they "might be filled with the knowledge of his will." When he comes to the end of the letter he tells them, as we have it in our text, that their friend *Epaphras* is praying that they might "stand perfect and complete in all the will of God," or, as another translation has it, "complete and fully assured."

The one is an advance upon the other. To know God's will is important, but never enough. We must get *into* it, and get *on* with it, surrender to it, stand within it. Where do you and I stand this day in relation to God's known will? Do we stand within it or outside of it?

Take something as mundane and "every-day" as your *job* or your *business.* Are you daily seeking His will, and are you surrendered to it, in this area of your life? As a Christian,

have you given full attention to the meaning of Paul's instruction to these Colossians: "And whatsoever ye do in
word or deed, do all in the name of the Lord Jesus" (3:17)?

Here is a boiler-room superintendent in a huge public
utility plant, with eighty men under him. They are tough
fellows, from a half-dozen different countries, full of tension
and temper. At times the situation is impossible. But prayer
convinces that Christian superintendent that the will of God
for him is to begin holding noon-hour "get-togethers." There
they bring up their sources of irritation and talk them out.
Result? The tensions have eased. Much of the profanity has
stopped, and the efficiency of the boiler-room operation has
been measurably stepped up.

Here is a young lawyer whose new client wants a divorce
in order to marry another man. The *legal* possibilities are
one thing. But, for this Christian lawyer, the *moral* possibilities and responsibilities are another thing. After an eve-
ning at home in prayer about it, he decides that God's will
for him is to tell her how she may save her marriage instead
of wrecking it. He does it. The home is preserved.

God's will is that you shall make a *Christian* approach to
everything in your business. Are you doing it?

Or take your *emotions,* which so largely run our lives, and
so often run them afoul. After saying, in verse 2 of chapter
3, "Set your affection on things above, not on things on the
earth," the Apostle becomes specific in verse 8, "Now ye also
put off all these: anger, wrath, malice," and the like. "Angry
and passionate outbreaks, ill-will," is the way Weymouth
translates it.

Colleen Townsend Evans, in the little basement dining
room used by herself and her husband while he was getting
his doctor's degree in Edinburgh, said to me with a chuckle,
"A psychiatrist here told me recently that it was good for all
of us to 'blow our tops' occasionally, that people who always
hold their temper become problem-cases." "But," she went
on, "I told him that I felt he didn't understand the Christian way — that actually I did 'let go' when provoking things

arose — I let go with prayer and love." She was right, of course. This emotional control is God's will for us.

Or take another area of your life — your *recreations* and *pleasures*. Are you seeking and following His will there? If it is true, as we saw a moment ago, that whatsoever we do, "in word or deed," we are to do "in the name of the Lord Jesus," then it follows that some forms of amusement are *out,* while others are *in.* In some sections of the country all college football games are opened not only with the singing of "The Star Spangled Banner" but with prayer as well. Say what you will about its being, for many, an empty form, the principle it represents is sound: if we are in His will, the fun we have is something upon which we can honestly ask God's blessing.

Charles Clayton Morrison has written a paragraph that I want you to hear with care: "Our commercialized entertainment system is producing a mentality of escape from the deeper and more ultimate issues of life. It blights mental spontaneity — the capacity to react critically and intelligently upon the subject matter which the system offers as entertainment. By undermining standards, it has broken down inhibitions. By breaking down inhibitions, it has corrupted taste. And by corrupting taste, it has stultified judgment. Thus the mind is left relatively inert, possessing its passive function of receiving sensations, but incapacitated to select, reject, or evaluate them."[1]

Yes, God's will has room in it for our recreations and relaxations. But it has no room in it for indulgences that blunt our moral sensitivities, that confuse our values, that cripple our influence over people of high-minded ideals or that otherwise cloud our view of the face of Jesus Christ.

So we might go on, looking now at this aspect of life and now at that, always asking the question: What is God's will for me here, and am I committed to it?

C. Come now to this: if understanding God's will is our problem and undertaking His will is our privilege, then

---

[1] *Can Protestantism Win America?* (New York: Harper and Brothers, 1948), p. 54.

seriously we must say that *undercutting His will is our peril.*
Two verses removed from our text there is a name I want
you to hear. It is "Demas." Paul says, "Luke, the beloved physician, and Demas, greet you." Luke, so far as we know,
never deviated from God's will for his life. But with Demas
it was different. A little later Paul wrote to his friend Timothy, and, with an ache in his heart, said, "Demas hath for-
saken me, having loved this present world" (II Tim. 4:10).

Just what was the fault in Demas' dedication? I do not
know. Just what was the coiled serpent of incomplete surrender that lay all the while in the heart of this Christian
man — waiting for the day when it would strike and poison
his whole life? I do not know. All we know is that it was
there.

Half-way surrender is the blight of Christian discipleship.
God is asking for *all,* and we want to "buy" Him off with
something less.

Edwin Orr, a servant of God with an international influence, has told in his book *Full Surrender* of the crisis that
came in his own Christian life when yieldedness to the
Divine Will was fractional rather than full. Kneeling one
night with a few friends in Belfast, he told the Lord that he
was willing to do anything, "anything to be surrendered and
filled." Then came an inner Voice, saying, "What about your
will?" Orr remarks that if he had been asked, What about
your besetting sins? he would have said, "Yes, once more I
confess them." But this was different: "What about your
will?"

Since he was taking a correspondence course on missions
given by the China Inland Mission, he told the Lord that
he was willing to be a missionary. But the Voice, not satisfied,
persisted. It asked about a certain romance that was blos-
soming in his life. Was he prepared to surrender *that* to
God's will? And Orr says that with his lips he could say
Yes, but with his heart he was saying No. That was the nub
and crux of the whole thing. That bit of withholding was
the undercutting of God's will in his life.

Only when he was willing honestly to confess that imper-

fect surrender as sin, and yield that final stronghold of the
self-life to Christ, did God fill him with the Holy Spirit and
release him for a ministry that has brought blessing to count-
less thousands around the world.

Later Dr. Orr was to write:

"Search me, O God, and know my heart today,
    Try me, O Saviour, and know my thoughts, I pray:
 See if there be some wicked way in me:
    Cleanse me from every sin and set me free.

"I pray Thee, Lord, to cleanse me now from sin:
    Fulfill Thy promise: make me pure within:
 Fill me with fire where once I burned with shame
    Grant my desire to magnify Thy name.

"Lord, take my life and make it all Thine own:
    I want to spend it serving Thee alone:
 Take all my will, my passion, self, and pride —
    I now surrender, Lord, in me abide."

The Epistle to Philemon

Philemon
LOVE'S SUPERLATIVES

Verses 9, 10. "For love's sake ... I beseech thee for my son Onesimus."

I. HISTORICAL SETTING. The link between Philemon and Colossians is close and extraordinary. Completely separate as to subject-matter and purpose, they nevertheless go together. All the available evidence indicates that they literally travelled together from Paul's place of imprisonment (presumably in Rome) to Colossae, the "church letter" carried by Tychicus and the "personal" note borne by a run-away slave, Onesimus, to his master, Philemon, whom he has wronged. The letter he is to deliver contains a masterpiece of a plea which Paul has drafted, the designed effect of which is to save Onesimus' life — and much more. The principal facts belonging to the background (as established by the letter or conjectured from it) are these:

1. Philemon was a well-regarded member of the Colossian church (as to location of the church, this is disputed by Goodspeed, who thinks that he and his house-church were in Laodicea).

2. Philemon, at some undisclosed time and place, had been converted through Paul's ministry and was well known to the apostle.

3. Philemon's slave, Onesimus, had stolen goods or money, or both, from him and had absconded, finally drifting to Rome.

4. At Rome Onesimus had met Paul, in unrecorded circumstances (Paul Minear suggests that they might have been incarcerated in the same prison), and by Paul is led to new life in Christ.

5. Though a warm friendship has developed between Paul and Onesimus, in which the younger man makes himself very helpful to the apostle, Paul knows that the only right course for Onesimus to follow is that of giving himself up to his master.

6. In what the famed Renan has called "a true little masterpiece in the art of letter-writing," Paul appeals to Philemon to receive back the slave who betrayed him, and to do it as a Christian. That is, he is to welcome him not as he would a repentant servant but as he would a fellow-Christian, which Onesimus now is.

It may be added that two or three modern expositors (John Knox being one of them) have challenged the traditional view set out in 6., their contention being that Paul's real, though delicately veiled, request was for Onesimus' emancipation and, that given, his return to Rome for Christian service at Paul's side.

II. EXPOSITORY MEANING

v. 2. "Apphia" is usually taken to be Philemon's wife.

"Archippus." Identity obscure; regarded by some as a son of Philemon and Apphia; Moule suggests that he was "mission-pastor at Colossae."

v. 6. The Greek text is difficult for the translator and obscure for the expositor — except in its general import. It is made lucid in the Revised Standard Version, though admittedly other translators would argue fine points in the rendering: "I pray that the sharing of your faith may promote the knowledge of all the good that is ours in Christ."

v. 7. For "bowels" read "hearts."

v. 8. "Enjoin" is better rendered "command," that is, in the exercise of apostolic authority.

"Convenient," in today's usage, is misleading; better given in the Revised Standard Version as "required."

v. 10. "Begotten in my bonds." Meaning, *"the spiritual son of my imprisonment."* Vincent's paraphrase is: "my son Onesimus, who has been converted through my instrumentality during my imprisonment."

v. 11. The whole verse is an example of charming word-play with, of course, completely serious intention. "Onesimus" was a slave-name, meaning *useful,* or *profitable.* With this in mind, Paul says, in effect, "Useful he is named, but in time past he was (I confess it) not useful, but useless; in future, however, he will be of great use to us both." The "profit" to Paul could take either (or both) of two forms: (1) as evidence of the success of his evangelistic and apostolic witness, (2) as a skillful and devoted helper in the midst of Paul's imprisonment.

v. 12. "I have sent." This tense is often used in letters, indicating that the writer is projecting himself forward to the time when the message arrives.

"Mine own bowels." A strong expression which, paraphrased, would be, "I am parting with my very heart" (Moffatt).

v. 13. Weymouth has a fine rendering of this verse, which is full of subtle charm: "It was my wish to keep him at my side for him to attend to my wants, as your representative, during my imprisonment for the gospel." Paul delicately assumes that Philemon, out of generous love and friendship, would have been glad to have it so.

v. 14. "Mind" has the force of *knowledge* and *consent.*

"Benefit" is well translated "kindness," thus giving the remainder of the verse the sense well brought out in the New English Bible, "so that your kindness may be a matter not of compulsion, but of your own free will."

v. 15. "Departed." "He was severed from you," is Moule's way of putting it. Paul's charm, both of thought and expression, is not easily captured in English. Moffatt has done extremely well with verses 15 and 16: "Perhaps this was why you and he were parted for awhile, that you might get him back for good, no longer a mere slave but something more than a slave — a beloved brother; especially dear to me but how much more to you as a man and as a Christian." A comma after "you" would have improved the punctuation.

v. 18. "Or oweth thee ought," is the phrase that supports

the view of Onesimus as having not only broken away from his master, but having also stolen from him.

"Put that on my account." This, together with what follows in the first part of verse 19, is Paul's way of saying, "Think of me as here and now obligating myself to reimburse you and, accordingly, writing out this I.O.U."

v. 19. "Albeit I do not say. . . . " Weymouth puts this in the form of a parenthesis and translates it: "I say nothing of the fact you owe me even your own self." The reference is to the part that Paul had in bringing Philemon to the knowledge of Christ.

v. 20. The Authorized Version is accurate enough, but archaic in style. The Phillips rendering captures excellently the intimately gracious and graceful manner in which Paul is expressing himself: "Now do grant me this favor, my brother — such an act of love will do my old heart good."

v. 21. "Thy obedience." That is, *the response that you in love will make to the loving request I am making of you.*

III. DOCTRINAL VALUE.
Professor Erdman's categorical, "It contains no statement of Christian doctrine," appears to be justified.

IV. PRACTICAL AIM.
The almost-private note (after all, the "church" is saluted in the introduction) was intended to bring about reconciliation between a Christian slave-owner, who has long been Paul's friend, and a run-away slave who is repentant and who, in his converted state, has become a valued friend of the imprisoned apostle. This, at any rate, is the primary aim of the letter. A more ulterior motive is ascribed to Paul by those who believe he was really working for the return of Onesimus by Philemon so that the apostle might have his continuing service.

HOMILETICAL FORM

Theme: "Love's Superlatives."

Introduction: Paul Tournier of Geneva, in his *Guilt and Grace* devotes a chapter to what he calls "Love with No Conditions." As a psychotherapist who is also a committed Christian, he makes no bones of using the resources of the Christian gospel in his work with patients. Although as a Christian he disagrees with Freud on points both religious and professional, he nevertheless holds Freud in great respect for some of his enduring insights. He believes, for example, that Freud has demonstrated how for many people emotional problems have grown out of a childhood fear of not being loved.

Tournier, agreeing, points out that well-meaning parents often say foolish and harmful things to misbehaving children. A mother will say, "I shan't love you any more because you have been a bad boy." In the first place, she does not really mean what she says; in the second place, if she does mean it, something has gone wrong with her mother-love. She has made her love conditional, the condition that the child is good.

The magnificence of God's love, the doctor goes on to point out, is that it is unconditional. No Bible writer has made more of this than Paul. "God commendeth his love towards us," he writes to the Romans, "in that, while we were yet sinners, Christ died for us." Had it been love for which we had to qualify — so much reform, so much penance, so much reparation, so many tears — it would not have been *grace*.

This, we must see, is the background for what Paul has to say to his friend Philemon in this gem of a letter, which is the only precious fragment of Paul's private correspondence that has been preserved for us.

"For love's sake . . . I beseech thee for . . . Onesimus."

To be sure, Onesimus had played truant to his master, Philemon. To be sure, he had been a rogue and a thief. To be sure, by the laws and customs of slavery then in effect, Philemon held the power of life and death over this wretched escapee.

"But Philemon, you are a Christian. As your Christian friend, I tell you that Onesimus has become a Christian. I have taken him to my heart and I want you to take him to yours. Receive him back — 'for love's sake.' "

Now out of this superbly moving — partly because superbly written — Paul-Onesimus-Philemon story I want to fashion four sentences about Christian love in each of which you will feel, I hope, the extravagance of the superlative.

A. Learn here, first of all, that *love has a ministry that serves the worst.*

Consider Onesimus. He was a slave in Colossae. Slaves were common as flies in the Roman Empire. But Phrygian slaves, of whom he was one, were notoriously poor slaves — more lazy, more insolent, than most. Whether it was cause or effect, the fact that they were more severely treated in the provinces of Asia Minor than they were in the other parts of the empire was known.

On this low starting point Onesimus had piled grave offenses of his own. His larceny and his treachery had put a thousand miles of distance between him and his master. Here he is now, among the human driftwood of the empire's capital. Some have surmised that for further offenses, committed while in Rome, he had been thrown into prison, and that *there* is where he had first come under the influence of Paul.

Say three things about him, if you wish:

He was *socially without status.* As might be expected, actual treatment of slaves throughout the empire varied from place to place, from family to family, but in no case were they regarded as having, in the normal sense, legal rights or social privileges.

He was *criminally without excuse.* In nobody's court could he have found anyone to defend him.

He was *personally without hope.* His youthfulness, far from relieving, only aggravated the grim fact that for him there was no future.

Yet love — Christ's love in this man Paul — took an interest in him. More, it took hold of him. It softened him, shattered him, remolded him, redeemed him. The details, alas, are hidden from us, but the end-effect is there for us to see: a man new-born in Christ — begotten in my bonds, as Paul so strikingly expresses it.

When I visit Jamaica, there is a presence I never see but *always* feel. The name of that "presence" is William Knibb. Is it a name that means anything to you?

From Bristol, England, Knibb had gone out to Jamaica as a missionary. This was at the end of the first quarter of the nineteenth century, when slavery was human slavery and was legally recognized and widely practiced in British possessions. So vile was the plight of the Jamaican slaves that Knibb felt that the gospel would make little progress while a professedly Christian government tolerated the system that had spawned such wretchedness. So besides preaching, Knibb began agitating. Here was a socio-economic situation in which marriage among the "blacks" was virtually unknown. So far as the system was concerned union between the sexes was for breeding purposes. And they were bred for the market. Even as children they would be sold as soon as their "limbs were set."

That Christ loved them William Knibb could not doubt. And in Christ Knibb loved them. On their behalf he fought the case of their freedom all the way to the British Parliament. In one of his impassioned pleas, while in England, he cried:

> "If I fail in arousing the sympathy of England, I will go back to Jamaica and call upon Him who hath made of one blood all nations upon the earth. And if I die without beholding the emancipation of my brethren and sisters in Christ, then, if prayer is permitted in heaven, I will fall at the feet of the Eternal, crying, 'Lord, open the eyes of Christians in England to see the evil of slavery and to banish it from the earth!'"

The people heard. Parliament heard. The Eternal heard. And the cruel yoke was broken — July 31, 1838.[1]

Ah, my soul, that ministry of love serves the worst. "Worst," at any rate in the eyes of men, and, not uncommonly, in their own eyes.

> "Love has a hem to her garment
> That trails in the very dust;
> It can reach the stains of the streets and lanes,
> And because it can, it must."

[1] Boreham, F. W., *A Bunch of Everlastings* (New York: Abingdon Press, 1920) p. 218.

B. Come now to our second sentence: *love has a courtesy that gains the most.* You cannot read Philemon without noting the captivating winsomeness that Paul displays as he makes his plea for the safety of Onesimus, who now will give himself up to his injured master.

Paul exhibits courtesy of *tone*: his words are fragrant with graciousness. Almost any of our more recent versions will convey this better than the stiff and archaic "King James." Let Phillips serve as an illustration.

Savor this from verse 5: "I have heard how you love and trust both the Lord Jesus himself and those who believe in him."

Or this from verse 7: "It is your love, my brother, that gives us such comfort and happiness, for it cheers the hearts of your fellow Christians."

Or this from verse 14: "I would do nothing without consulting you first, for if you have a favor to give me, let it be spontaneous and not forced from you by circumstances."

Or this from verse 17: "You and I have so much in common, haven't we? Then do welcome him as you would welcome me."

Or this from verse 21: "As I send this letter I know you'll do what I ask."

What elegance and graciousness of tone!

What is more important, however, is the courtesy of *temper* that explains the tone. It would be untrue to say that Paul's approach to Philemon was not a *studied* one. It was. But it would be equally untrue to say that it was not an *honest* approach. Paul did feel this way toward his friend. David one time complained regarding a traitorous enemy — perhaps his own son Absalom — that "his words were softer than oil, yet were they drawn swords" (Ps. 55:21). There was nothing akin to such duplicity in what Paul was sharing with Philemon.

There is value in being an artist with words, but that value sinks near the vanishing point if there is no deep, rich integrity to give backing to the artistry.

In a delightful biographical sketch of Henry Drummond

the late F. W. Boreham refers to him as the "Prince of But-
tonholers," because he was always engaging people in conversation, showing interest in them and in their affairs,
revelling in their joys and sympathizing in their sorrows,
and, above all, eager to introduce them to his best friend,
Jesus Christ. Referring to this conversational evangelism
Boreham says that Drummond became "a past-master of the
art. He made every man he tackled feel that he loved him,
and he made his companion *feel* that he loved him for the
simple reason that *he really did.*"

Without that "he really did" courtesy is a veneer. And the
gaudier it is, the shoddier. Courtesy, let it be remembered,
is always better than incivility or asperity or brutality.

And courtesy is nearly always better than *authority*, especially when you are dealing with adults and older children.
Paul was too shrewd a student of people not to know this.
It was only in extreme cases of irregularity or irresponsibility
that he wielded the big stick of his apostolic authority. With
Philemon he says, "And although I could rely on my authority in Christ and dare to order you to do what I consider right, I am not doing that. No, I am appealing to that
love of yours" (vs. 8, 9, Phillips).

Could Philemon resist that? Not unless he had a stony
heart.

C. Let us reach now for our third sentence: *love has an
honesty that will not take advantage in the least.*

The nub of what I have to say here is found in the simple
words of verse 12, which Phillips renders, "I am sending him
back to you."

"You didn't capture him. You had no idea where he was.
You probably had little hope of ever laying eyes on him
again. Besides, I have found him extremely useful, now that
he too is a transformed man and a follower of our Lord,
and I should have kept him right here if I had followed my
personal desires." All this Paul is saying in substance.

But he is saying something more! "I am sending him back
to you — and he is in full agreement with the plan — because

he has wronged you. Although I know God has forgiven him and he has become a new man, he must 'face the music.' After all, he legally belongs to you. Surely not one of us wants to take God's foregiveness as a device to escape the consequences of wrongdoing. I am sure that you will forgive him, as God has, but that must be your decision as a Christian."

It is incredibly easy for us to turn what the New Testament calls love — Christ's love (in source) possessing us (in effect) — into a lovely, remote ideal or into a saccharine, ineffectual sentiment. A New Testament scholar like C. H. Dodd regrets that we ever tried to translate the Greek *agape* since, in his view, it is untranslatable. His own words are worth repeating: "It is not primarily an emotion or affection; it is primarily an active determination of the will." The distinction is a sound one, particularly if we think of the "determination," not as teeth-gritting effort of our own, but a posture, a stance, a controlling attitude induced by the Holy Spirit of God within us.

Sentimental love cuts corners, evades issues, dotes on coziness and dislikes being upset by challenges, cries over spilled milk in the kitchen and cares little about working conditions or health conditions at the dairy, can do a rhapsody over "humanity" but is indifferent to "people" (except those who serve them well or keep their place). Sentimental love sings "Jesus Paid It All" and lets the butcher or the baker or the plumber go unpaid.

John Mitchell of Dallas, president of a manufacturing company by that name, has written a book called *The Christian in Business*. One of his stories is about a young man who, while in college, had a part-time night job with the company. Because other men on the night-shift were trusted college fellows, no supervision was in effect. A year after one of the men had left the plant and moved to another state, Mr. Mitchell received a letter from him. It read, in part:

"Dear Mr. Mitchell:
The past few weeks and months have been the most thrilling in my Christian experience. . . . But along with this richness of

fellowship has come the searchlight of the Word.... On several occasions, when, as night-time employee of the John E. Mitchell Co., I came to work, I punched in at the time clock, then left to do other things of my own choosing, and returned hours later to punch out and go home. This was just plain stealing.... The Lord has already graciously forgiven me, and at this time I ask your forgiveness."

Now if the letter had stopped there, how much respect would Mr. Mitchell have had for all these unctuous words of testimony? It did not stop there! It went on:

"My guess is that the amount (to be paid back) would be about $60.... As soon as I am financially able, I will send you the money."

Mr. Mitchell's reply was gracious and forgiving, but it made no offer to cancel the obligation. When the money came, the check was endorsed over to the young man's church and returned to him. The whole transaction, you see, was saved from vapid sentimentality by downright Christian honesty.

But I am not content to let this issue of love's honesty and honor rest with an illustration as simple and conventional as this.

Take a much more subtle illustration. In company with Bob Pierce of World Vision I was spending some hospitable hours in the residence of a United States official in Indonesia. Our hostess told me a moving story about the turn of events in the life of her Louisiana-born husband, by which he was suddenly shorne of his white-and-Negro philosophy. You know what that philosophy is.— though it would be a serious mistake to confine it to that beloved part of our nation that lies below the Mason-Dixon Line. James Dabbs, himself a Southerner, has described it as a philosophy which proposes to treat Negroes decently and even affectionately as long as they stay in "their place." Apparently, says Dabbs,

"there is something attached to every Negro which is not attached to every white man: the idea of place.... We like him in his place. The liking is a bonus for staying there. We don't have to give the white man any bonus for staying in his place, the place itself is the bonus. The Negro's place being unattractive, has to carry a bonus with it. Consequently, white people like or dislike other white people for purely individual or personal reasons. With one exception: if a white man, for some fool reason, gets out of his place — fails, that is, to keep the Negro at the proper distance, in the place he belongs in, where he can be liked — we bestow upon him our deepest dislike.

We like any Negro, then, just so long as he remains in the inferior position to which he has been assigned, as actual or potential servant. We do not like him as a man; indeed, we seldom see the solid, living man beneath the abstraction servant."[2]

Forgive this interjection, but that was the philosophy of race relations which our host had been soaking up from infancy. But then came the day when he went away to law school at a distant university. After graduation he made a visit to the old homestead, a delightful plantation that had been in the family from slavery days. One day a Negro employee, who had been with the family for decades, who had watched fondly as "Mar'se Jim" (our host) grew up, came to him. Shyly and haltingly he told "Jim" that he needed some advice. His son was in trouble with the "law." The father felt that the case was not as serious as the plaintiffs were alleging, and told *why* he felt this way. What should be done? Fresh from a law school, Jim said to him, sympathetically, "Henry [I have forgotten whether this was the name or not], if these are the facts, you've got to have a lawyer," quite forgetting that no lawyer in the region would take his case.

What happened in the next thirty seconds changed Jim for life! He said the old man stood there, speechless, an indescribably quizzical look on his gentle old face. And these were the words with which he broke the silence: "Mar'se Jim, has you fo'gotten? I ain't a *man* — like you!"

In that second, stunningly bright in its sudden illumination, Jim Baird knew in his heart of hearts that the "system" was wrong. From that day on, let others do what they might, for Jim Baird to put love and honesty together meant to break with the old pattern.

The house, I may add, in which "Jim" and "Mary" were

---

[2] *The Southern Heritage* (Alfred A. Knopf, Inc.), pp. 177, 178.

then living was a social and spiritual sanctuary where God-hungry people — Indonesians, Malayans, Britons, Americans from the USA — were meeting together to sing and pray and find guidance for their Christian witness in Indonesia's capital.

Love has a ministry that serves the worst, a courtesy that gains the most, an honesty that will not compromise in the least.

I do want to point out one thing more.

D. Love has *an expectancy that looks for the best.*

How will Philemon receive this extraordinary request of Paul's? Well, Paul will not have it any other way than that his friend will "come through."

There must be a psychology of the Holy Ghost, and here it is in verse 21: "As I send you this letter I know you'll do what I ask — I believe, in fact, *you'll do more.*" (Phillips)

There is love's expectancy in full bloom — looking for the best.

In the long run we get out of people — forgive this crude way of putting it — just about what we expect of them.

Take a child, for example. If he is treated negatively, pessimistically, told frequently that he is lazy, or untidy, or "dumb," or clumsy, the child's personality output will diminish rather than increase. The same thing goes for the moral virtues in the child. Let him be constantly suspected of lying, or cheating, or stealing, or bullying, and the chances are that the parents will *get* what they are suspecting.

Christ's love in us is incredibly creative, incorrigibly positive, incessantly expectant. Is this not what Paul brings out superbly in the famous Hymn of Love? Love "beareth all things, believeth all things, hopeth all things, endureth all things" (I Cor. 13:7).

At the end of the eighteenth century a man by the name of William Wilberforce, a hunch-backed member of Parliament, was fighting what at times appeared to be an almost single-handed battle against the institution of slavery in the empire. Even though he had a heart as brave as was ever possessed by a knight in shining armor, he was not above assaults of discouragement. On a February day in 1791, the aged John Wesley, being only a week away from his death, wrote Wilberforce a letter in which he said:

"If God be for you, who can be against you? Are all of them (men and devils) stronger than God? Oh! 'Be not weary in well-doing.' Go on, in the name of God, and in the power of His might, till even American slavery (the vilest that ever saw the sun) shall vanish before it.... That He who has guided you, from your youth up, may continue to strengthen you in this and all things, is the prayer of, dear sir, your affectionate servant, John Wesley."

Who can measure the lift that such a message brought to Wilberforce? Wesley believed in him, believed in the cause for which he was battling, believed, above all, in the power and the purpose of the God they both were serving. "Affectionately yours!"

Love looking for the best!

What happened when Onesimus, bearing Paul's letter, got back to Colossae and gave himself up to his old master, Philemon?

I do not know. And yet I am sure! There is no record to support knowledge. There is only this hunch in my heart to support certainty.

Onesimus stands while Philemon reads. No cringing on the one hand; no arrogance on the other. Just the quiet humility of a penitent whom Christ has received.

Philemon finishes. Looks at Onesimus, head to foot. He glances again at the letter. "Receive him back.... not merely a slave ... but ... as a brother Christian."

Ah, there was the fuse whose delayed action would one day blow the institution of slavery to bits.

"A brother Christian!"

Philemon smiles. Paul has his wish. Christ's love has its way. And Onesimus receives his kiss. The kiss — in Eastern fashion — of reconciliation, acceptance! Legend has it that Onesimus was one day made bishop.

"For love's sake!"

BIBLIOGRAPHY

Barth, Karl, *The Epistle to the Philippians,* London: SCM Press, Ltd., 1947.

Beare, F. W., *A Commentary on the Epistle to the Philippians,* New York: Harper & Brothers, 1959.

Buttrick, George A., *Philemon* (The Interpreter's Bible), Nashville: Abingdon Press, 1955.

Carson, Herbert M., *Colossians and Philemon,* (Tyndale New Testament Commentaries), Grand Rapids, Michigan: Wm. B. Eerdmans Publishing Company, 1960.

Caffin, B. C., *Philippians and Colossians* (Pulpit Commentary), New York: Funk and Wagnalls Co.

Cragg, Herbert W., *The Sole Sufficiency of Jesus Christ,* "Colossians," London: Marshall, Morgan & Scott, 1961.

Davies, Rupert E., *A Colony of Heaven,* "Philippians," London: The Epworth Press, 1958.

Eadie, John, *A Commentary on the Colossians,* Edinburgh: T. & T. Clark, 1884.

Greenway, Alfred L., *The Epistle to the Philippians,* Grand Rapids, Michigan: Baker Book House, 1957.

Guthrie, Thomas, *Christ and the Inheritance of the Saints,* Edinburgh: Adam and Charles Black, 1858.

Harrison, Norman B., *His in Joyous Experience,* "Philippians," Chicago: Moody Press, 1926.

Hunter, Archibald M., *Galatians, Ephesians, Philippians, Colossians* (Layman's Bible Commentary, Vol. 22), Richmond: John Knox Press, 1959.

Johnstone, Robert, *The Epistle of Paul to the Philippians,* Grand Rapids, Michigan: Baker Book House, 1955 (reprint).

Jones, Maurice, *The Epistle of St. Paul to the Colossians,* London: Society for Promoting Christian Knowledge, 1923.

————, *The Epistle to the Philippians* (Westminster Commentaries), London: Methuen & Co., Ltd., 1918.

Kelly, William, *Lectures on the Epistle of Paul the Apostle to the Philippians,* London: G. Morrish.

Knox, John, *Philemon* (The Interpreter's Bible), Nashville: Abingdon Press, 1955.

Lightfoot, J. B., *St. Paul's Epistle to the Philippians,* London: Macmillan and Co., 1879.

————, *St. Paul's Epistles to the Colossians and to Philemon,* London: Macmillan and Co., 1892.

Mac Leod, G. Preston, *Colossians* (The Interpreter's Bible), Nashville: Abingdon Press, 1955.

Martin, Ralph P., *The Epistle of Paul to the Philippians* (Tyndale New Testament Commentary), Grand Rapids, Michigan: Wm. B. Eerdmans Publishing Company, 1959.

Meyer, F. B., *The Epistle to the Philippians,* London: The Religious Tract Society, 1929.

Moule, H. C. G., *Colossian Studies,* London: Hodder and Stoughton, 1898.

————, *Philippian Studies,* London: Hodder and Stoughton, 1908.

Newland, Henry, *The Epistle of St. Paul to the Philippians,* London: J. H. and James Parker, 1860.

Noble, Frederick A., *Discourses on the Epistle of Paul to the Philippians,* New York: Fleming H. Revell Co., 1896.

Plummer, Alfred, *A Commentary on St. Paul's Epistle to the Philippians,* London: Roxburghe House, 1919.

Radford, Lewis B., *The Epistle to the Colossians and the Epistle to Philemon* (Westminster Commentaries), London: Methuen & Co., Ltd., 1931.

Rainy, Robert, *The Epistle to the Philippians* (The Expositor's Bible), New York: A. C. Armstrong and Son, 1893.

Robertson, A. T., *Paul and the Intellectuals,* Nashville: Broadman Press, (Rev. 1959).

Schmidt, O. H., *St. Paul Shows Us How,* "Colossians," St. Louis: Concordia Publishing House, 1950.

Scott, Ernest F., *Philippians* (The Interpreter's Bible), Nashville: Abingdon Press, 1955.

Simcox, Carroll E., *They Met at Philippi,* New York: Oxford University Press, 1958.

Trentham, Charles A., *The Shepherd of the Stars,* Nashville: Broadman Press, 1962.

Vaughan, C. J., *Lectures on St. Paul's Epistle to the Philippians,* London: Macmillan and Co., 1882.

Vincent, Marvin, *International Critical Commentary,* Edinburgh: T. & T. Clark, 1897.

White, R. E. O., *Apostle Extraordinary,* Grand Rapids: Wm. B. Eerdmans Publishing Company, 1962.

Wicks, Robert R., *Philippians* (The Interpreter's Bible), Nashville: Abingdon Press, 1955.